Your Glasses Are on TOP of Your Head

Joy–

Brenda Elsagher

Your Glasses Are on TOP of Your Head

Tales of Life, Longevity, and Laughter

BRENDA ELSAGHER

Print ISBN 13: 978-1-63489-005-2
e-book ISBN 13: 978-1-63489-006-9

Library of Congress Control Number: 2015947644

Printed in the United States of America
First Printing: 2015
19   18   17   16   15   5   4   3   2   1

Cover and interior design by James Monroe Design, LLC.

Wise Ink, Inc.
837 Glenwood Avenue,
Minneapolis, Minnesota 55405

wiseinkpub.com
To order, visit itascabooks.com or call 1-800-901-3480.
Reseller discounts available.

Dedication

To my dear friend, Sherry Wenborg: You have been a nurturing mother, sister, confidante, gentle pusher, and greatest supporter for the forty years we have been friends. I love you.

Where would I be without my girlfriends? To all of you dear women in my life, grade school buddies to the more recent, you are each dear to me. Your wisdom, humor, and presence in my life has challenged me, humored me, comforted me, and lifted me up as well as rooted me and shaped the person I am. Thanks for your love and the precious time you've spent with me in my life.

Additional books by Brenda Elsagher:

If the Battle Is Over, Why Am I Still in Uniform?

I'd Like to Buy a Bowel Please!

Bedpan Banter

It's In the Bag and Under the Covers

Available at Amazon.com
LivingandLaughing.com

Acknowledgments

To the many volunteers who dedicated time and energy for the Humor Academy program through the Association of Applied and Therapeutic Humor (AATH). Thanks for the amazing work you do to help all people learn how to apply the use of therapeutic humor in education, health care, family, work, and play. I also thank the many legends who could see this important subject as necessary to study, and also do projects in order to produce evidence-based research. Your science, knowledge, and willingness to share have been instrumental in changing the world, one smile at a time. You founders, facilitators, and leaders encouraged me to do a project using my humor, and here it is. I have enjoyed my affiliation with you, and look forward to more years ahead.

Thanks to those of you who were objective readers who read and rated each story, and discussed them with me: Sue Brown, Gail Fuad, Pat Turgeon, Sherry Wenborg, Betty Wogensen, and Pat Walsh. Your time with me, and the stories, was invaluable.

I also appreciated the focus group of women in their fifties, sixties, and seventies who spent the day with me defining the purpose of this book, and the great dialogue to explore if it was possible to age hilariously. Thanks for straightening me out on the subject. While we do have moments of hilarity as we age, the "working title," *Aging Hilariously*, was an overstatement.

Brenda Elsagher

Your discussion made me think differently on the theme of this book, as well as its new title. Thank you: Janie Jasin, Mary Ellen Russell, Deb Tompkins, Sherry Wenborg, Grace Lee, Chris Heeter, Maxine Jeffris, Sue Brown, and Joyce Elsen.

Many thanks to the contributors of this book for sharing your stories on the perspective of aging. My hope is that we continue to experience the humor in our lives, laced with laughter, adventure, and contentment, as we pass through the years day by day.

Thanks to Louie Anderson, Janie Jasin, Terri Harris, Chris Heeter, Rox Tarrant, Monica Sausen, and Sherry Wenborg who contributed in other ways by listening and offering suggestions.

Thanks to James Monroe Design for the fun cover design.

Thanks to Matt Xi Photography, and also the front cover model, Pam Huck.

Thanks to Hollister Incorporated for your constant support.

Thanks to professional editor Connie Anderson and Wise Ink Creative Publishing for your wisdom.

To my husband Bahgat, thanks for your patience and help with technical difficulties, bringing me tea, and leaving me alone for hours at a time so I could get this book done.

Contents

SECTION I: FUNNY OBSERVATIONS

SECTION II: MEMORY LAPSE FOLLIES

SECTION III: COVERT BODY CHANGES

SECTION IV: FAMILY WISDOM

SECTION V: LEARNING ADVENTURES

SECTION VI: INTIMACY FUN

SECTION VII: HEALTH AND HAPPINESS

Your Glasses Are on Top of Your Head

Introduction

"Growing old is not for sissies!" said the salty 102-year-old woman as she rolled her walker into my salon. She was the fourth generation of a family I had known for twenty-five years. I had cut hair for the other three generations, and now I was getting to know the matriarch. Her daughter, now in her seventies, had been a funny woman until a botched surgery left her with unrelenting facial pain. I felt it was a personal challenge to get these two women to laugh out loud during my interactions with them, even if only for a short time.

Somehow early on in my life I found that humor could help distract one from pain, whether it was physical or emotional, and later I found it could even distract from spiritual pain, too. I experienced all those things myself, and could sense when it might be appropriate to attempt to make someone laugh, even in a very sad or uncomfortable time.

My dad modeled some of this intuition, as he always found a way to make a visiting friend of one of the eight kids feel welcome—especially the quiet ones. Dad would find a way to make her laugh, and ultimately our friend would relax a little, and then my dad might ask her questions about herself, and usually find something else to tease her about. This taught me a couple of things early on—*tease people to set a level of comfort, and use humor to relax situations.*

You can get people to endear to you if you ask them about their lives and get to know them.

Those were invaluable tools I use to this day. Besides, I'm genuinely interested in learning about how others think, what is precious to them, or maybe what motivates them. Perhaps this is why this is my fourth anthology; I love collaborating with others.

Throughout my earlier career as a hairstylist, I found lots of opportunities to reduce my stress using humor, especially when I was running behind. "You are on time and I am not. I will reward your patience with a beautiful style just for you. Then prepare yourself. When you get home, your husband won't be able to resist you and your hair will most likely be tousled."

During the last ten years of owning my second hair salon, I was also learning to write comedy and perform in comedy clubs. One thing led to another, and I was putting less time in the salon, and instead traveling a couple times a month to speak. It took about six years for me to realize speaking was a serious path to explore; then I made a new business card offering to speak.

I had been writing, and it was time to fully commit to the career based on humor, particularly focusing on humor *through adversity*. I used all the skills I had practiced and learned about communication and took them on the road, and began doing comedy and speaking for huge groups of people.

Laughing . . . as Death Announces Itself

One day a woman called and told me she had just read my first book, *If the Battle Is Over, Why Am I Still in Uniform?* She said she could relate a lot to what I went through as a colon cancer survivor, except with one difference: her diagnosis was terminal. She was a couple years younger than me, and our kids were similar in age. When she asked me to speak at her support group close to my home, I didn't hesitate.

The first person I met in the group said, "I don't know how I can possibly laugh at anything about colon cancer. I lost my beautiful daughter to it last year."

I knew this might be difficult, but I did the best I could, and he thanked me afterward for helping him see he could laugh at awful things, and that cancer wouldn't have so much power over him anymore. He said he wished his wife had come with him.

Teresa, the woman who had asked me to speak, wanted to keep in touch, and so we made plans for lunch at her favorite Mexican restaurant nearby. A couple months went by; she invited me to visit and showed me her scrapbooking room, and I learned how dedicated she was to this hobby. She had been making huge scrapbooks for everyone in her family, and they were beautiful. I learned she had several trips planned for each of her children. She allowed them to take one day off a month from school to hang out with her and was doing a lot of fun things, creating happy memories while she still felt good, hoping beyond statistics that she would survive. She lived with purpose, also took trips with friends and sisters, living life with gusto and making more memory books from those trips.

When I ran into her at a craft boutique, we both celebrated that she was still alive. We set time for some margaritas, and again I enjoyed her company very much. I would call and tease her when she answered the phone, saying something charming like, "Well, you are still alive!" It sounds crass in writing, but it was the weird right thing for me to say, and for us to laugh about because it was her ultimate worry. It was a couple more months before I heard from her again.

"Brenda, I've got something to tell you, and then a favor to ask of you."

"Okay friend, what is it?"

"We just got back from the doctors, and the cancer is now in my brain. I won't have much time left, months only, and there's something I want to discuss. I want you to give the eulogy at my funeral."

"Wow, Teresa, I know the cancer must have really gone to your brain. You want someone from your family who's known you for a long time to do this at your funeral, not a friend you barely know. We've only seen each other a few times and there's a lot I don't know about you. I'm honored, but I don't think I am the right person."

"Brenda, I've been thinking about this for a long time. I knew this time was coming. This is why I know this is a big favor. You will have to spend some time with my family and me, getting to know me. I want people to laugh at my funeral, so I want you to do this because you are funny, and I know you'll send them away with a special gift."

"What's that, Teresa?"

"I want you to tell them how important it is for them to get their colonoscopies. You and I were unusual because we were diagnosed so young. As you said in your talk at the support group, it is your mission to educate people on this. You've got to urge them to follow through as a last word from me. Can you do this? Will you do this for me?"

"How can I refuse? Are you sure?"

"You will give the perfect eulogy, I know it."

"Okay, when shall I come over?"

Your Glasses Are on Top of Your Head

Over the next couple months, I went to Teresa's quite a bit, met her kids, got to know her husband, saw the projects she had done over the years, looked at all the scrapbooks she had made, talked about her things left undone so far, and talked about her funeral.

She had less and less energy, and had been sleeping for two days and not eating or drinking much when I sat by her bed. I wanted to say goodbye again, as I had some speeches to give out of town. Suddenly, she sat up in her bed, looked right at me, and said, "Brenda, have I done enough?"

I answered, "Oh my gosh girl, I would say so. You've packed in special days with your kids, you've traveled to many great places, you've scrapbooked everything that walked by—I think you've done enough."

She smiled, and lay back down and went to sleep again. A couple days later she died, and the family called me. They even changed the funeral date to accommodate my schedule because they knew what Teresa wanted. I was honored to give her eulogy.

I prayed a lot for the right words on the day of her funeral. A mixture of funny stories and poignant moments about Teresa and her family described a life well lived. I knew as I delivered my eulogy, it was the most important talk I had given in my life. Over three hundred people were present, and the only ones I knew were her family: this eulogy was for them. Of course, I delivered her gift to everyone sitting there, and we laughed as we remembered Teresa. I was humbled to be at this solemn occasion using my gifts of curiosity, intuition, and humor in difficult situations.

Enjoying Our Life—Today

As I age, I realize the importance of good friends and family, and I must continue to meet my desires to travel and see new things. It's okay to be adventurous and curious about people and places, and even to be downright silly at times. In so many ways, I feel like life is just beginning. I care less about what other people think about my choices in life, and more about using my hours on projects that are good for my character and my sense of joy and giving. I know it's not too late to try things I have long put off.

At our wedding, our soloist sang a John Lennon song taken from the poem, "Grow Old Along with Me; the Best Is Yet to Be." I had always interpreted those words to mean to age as a couple, and enjoy it more as you age—and it would be good. Perhaps it might mean I am responsible for myself as I get older, to make my own life the best it can be. Whether it's volunteering my time with animals, trying out a new recipe, joining a book club, or gardening, it's something to stimulate me, my brain, and my interactions with others.

I think it might be true that we must remain open and willing to challenge our thinking and try new things—after all, *the best is yet to be.*

Section I
Funny Observations

"And keep a sense of humor. It doesn't mean you have to tell jokes. If you can't think of anything else, when you're my age, take off your clothes and walk in front of a mirror. I guarantee you'll get a laugh."

—ART LINKLETTER

Maiden to Crone

LISA MILLHAM

I found a four-inch-long gray hair growing out of my chest this week. It's just the latest in a long line of things I knew would be coming as I become a lady of "a certain age," but I've never really reconciled myself to it. I started noticing black mustache hairs about a year ago, and over the last summer, became the bearded lady as the coarse hair now growing out of my chin and my sideburns rivaled my husband's. I knew we girls start to get hairier after menopause, but I wish someone had warned me: I am apparently descended from a long line of werewolves.

I've recently come to terms with the fact I am no longer the ingénue, or the sweet, spunky heroine I write about in my books. I write fantasy aimed at a crowd now much younger than me, and the stories I have been writing deal with the maidenly aspect of the female lifespan. In doing so, I've recently started to wonder if it's my attempt to remain in touch with my youthful side—the one who still has the mind and heart of a much younger woman, even if the body is starting to droop in formerly perky places.

I am beginning to leave the motherly aspect of womanhood behind as I am past childbearing years, due to medical reasons and now that my own children, born later in my life, are rapidly approaching adulthood.

I am now becoming the crone. The word "crone" conjures images of wrinkled old women with sagging breasts, and yes, there's hair growing out of their chins as they loom ominously, draped in funereal cloaks and leaning on a crooked staff. While the sagging and hairy conditions apply to me, I do not currently own a staff, and I have too much dandruff to wear black. If I loom ominously, it's usually because I've forgotten what I was about to do, or I'm not wearing my glasses and have to get really close to you.

In days of yore, the crone aspect of women referred to wisdom, rather than physical condition or appearance. Elder women were looked up to as a source of knowledge as stories, skills, and hard-earned lessons were passed down from mother to daughter to granddaughter. They remembered the old ways and superstitions protecting the family from things that go bump in the night. They helped deliver babies to bring life into the world, or sat with the dying as they left to go on to the next.

In my other work as a hospice nurse, I have learned a great deal about the aging process, and how inside every elderly woman I care for beats the heart of a girl.

I need no proof, because I can feel it in myself. Inside the body that appears to be aging more quickly than I anticipated is a mind that still loves fairy tales, superheroes, and magic. At times this mind resents having to be a grown-up, and do grown-up things like work and pay bills. This mind also is starting to worry about driving at night because I don't see as well. My formerly steel-trap thought processes are now more like one of those doors that shuts quickly at first, then sighs slowly closed. I know the answers, I really do. If my brain were a computer screen, it would display the little expanding line saying, "Buffering . . ." The information is there, but it just takes a while to come to the surface.

Then there's the bladder that wakes me up two or three times a night to pee. Don't get me started on the leaking-when-I-laugh-or-sneeze bit. I feel my age in the way other people react to me. Having made a mid-life career change, I should be used to it by now, as most of my nursing supervisors are younger than me by several years. The new nurses coming on are so very young. Suddenly, I'm the one who's supposed to know everything. Do I just radiate grown-up vibes now? It must be the gray hair.

I'm really not lamenting the fact that my life is taking its natural course. We all grow old, and there's no stopping it, and no amount of anti-wrinkle cream, silicone injections, or vitamins is going to change this fact. My deepest wish is that I will grow old gracefully and eccentrically. I want to be that elderly woman with long gray hair and wildly colored clothes who doesn't give two hoots about what other people think of her lifestyle. I want to retain my memories, and watch them over and over again like a Lord of the Rings marathon. I want to continue to make new memories until the day I die.

At the relatively young age of thirty-nine, the reality of how short life is was driven home by a diagnosis that was only supposed to happen to "old people." I think this experience caused me to take a hard look at what happiness is. My growing older is a gift denied to many people of my young age who were diagnosed with colorectal cancer before the age of fifty. I can thank this horrible event in my life for prodding me to reach for my dream of becoming a published author, and to continue to turn my dream into a career for my dotage.

"Dotage" is a fancy word for old age, but I found an alternative definition to be "second childhood." Now that's something I can sink my still-all-original teeth into. Childhood as an adult by necessity will lack the innocence my first childhood did. For instance, I know now I can't run naked through lawn sprinklers at my age. I can still stare in wonder at the night sky, or stay up all night reading a book under the covers with a flashlight. I can still develop book-crushes on the characters in the books I read.

I plan on staying myself, and not letting old age define my parameters. My joints may be getting more painful, but ibuprofen is plentiful, and I can deal with stiff joints as long as my mind remains flexible and I can still stretch my imagination. My hair may be getting streaked with silver, but I still have hair.

Moving from maiden to mother to crone is really all one journey for me. The maiden parts of my heart are still there, and the motherly parts of me will forever live in my relationship with my children, long into the crone phase. I can see her there in the mirror, not so far away, but beckoning me with a gnarled finger bedecked with cool jewelry and sparkly nail polish as if to say, "Come on, it'll be fun. Who cares if your boobs tuck into your waistband now? Live it up!"

I kind of like her. But we're going to have to talk about the moustache.

The iPad Dilemma

Judith Huck

My husband purchased an iPad for me to take on my trip to Europe with my girlfriends. This way I could communicate with him, and be able to look up anything that might enhance our touring experience.

The iPad was sitting on the counter when I spilled a glass of water on the same counter. Horrors! I knew the water would not be good for the iPad. I quickly dried it, and then turned it on. Drops of water remained inside the iPad. I took the iPad to the nearest Apple Store, and waited in line to see someone from the support team.

He didn't even look at the iPad. "Water? It'll cost $250 for a reconditioned one; I'll set up an appointment for next week for you to pick one up."

"$250?" I went home.

I Googled how to remove the water droplets. I got the rice out of the cupboard, put it in a large plastic bin, enclosed the iPad in two plastic bags, and placed it in the bin of rice. After two days, I opened the iPad and the water droplets remained. I Googled again.

This time I went to Michael's craft store and purchased ten pounds of silica. Again, I wrapped the iPad in two plastic bags and placed it in the bin of silica. While the iPad was drying, many family members had come and gone. I asked each one of them how to remove water from the iPad. They looked at the plastic bin, and said they could offer no other suggestions. This time I left the iPad in the bin for one week.

When I removed the iPad, I turned it on, and the water droplets remained. It was time for a professional before I would spend the $250. My husband took the iPad to another tech place, waited in line, and told his story. They cleaned the iPad with a dry cloth, turned it on, asked my husband if these were the water droplets on the screen he was concerned about.

"Yes, that's the water. We can't get it out."

"Sir, this is called the wallpaper. This is not actually water in your iPad; it just looks like it. I suggest you choose wallpaper with flowers." Then he proceeded to show him how to choose another background so we would not have the same problem again. Since then, we have taken many classes, received more training, and hopefully will be more tech savvy in the future.

White Hair

BRENDA ELSAGHER

When my children were under six years old, they hadn't yet grasped the concept of their grandparents having their own names. They just knew them as Grandpa and Grandma. Somehow along the way, they latched on to the idea that people with white or gray hair were all called Grandpa and Grandma.

We were leaving our appointment at the clinic when we got into the elevator with an elderly couple. They were interested in my children, asked them the usual questions about their names and ages, general chitchat. At the end of the brief elevator ride, as we parted, both of my kids cheerfully said, "Goodbye, Grandpa and Grandma."

The X-Deficiency

Joyce Saltman

I love being married. My husband is a great friend, and is handsome, bright, loving, and fun to be around. He embodies all the qualities I had on the list I created the year after my first husband died of cancer. He wakes up happy every morning, goes to sleep with a smile on his face, and spends his days enjoying life. However, from my experience, he also suffers from one simple malady: the X-deficiency.

Have you ever wondered why men have such problems performing seemingly simple tasks? Anticipating needs is beyond them; knowing a payment will be required in moments is not enough to encourage them to have the wallet out or charge card in hand. They see no apparent need to remove keys from a pocket in order to open the car or front door. In heavy traffic, seeing brake lights illuminated for miles ahead does not signal the need to slow down, nor does the advent of elderly guests having difficulty hearing indicate a need to speak more slowly or loudly. In addition, spots on pants or worn areas on leather shoes appear to be invisible to their eye. They can't seem to find food containers or beverages stored behind another item, and if labels on drugs or spices are facing the rear of the cabinet, the container is also considered "missing." Add to these factors: when a male is asked to put the wash into the dryer, he will place the entire contents of the washing machine into the dryer and leave them there, unless specifically instructed to turn on the dryer.

A female security agent at the White Plains airport summed it up perfectly: "As soon as a man gets married, he is in assisted living."

I am fairly convinced the scientific explanation for all of these anomalies is the X-deficiency.

Women, having been blessed with a double dose of X's, seem to be proficient in all the noted areas, as well as others too numerous to mention. In the absence of the extra X, men demonstrate the skills of young children and the helplessness of lost kittens. Clearly, given that the X-deficiency renders most men "untrainable," the job of the womenfolk is to love, cherish, and care for the weaker sex, understanding that God created all men equal, but women superior.

So despite these few little flaws, I would never want to see a world without them.

Oh, Tannenbaum

Red Lyons

At Christmastime, I can easily slip into a 34th-street mood, and I like to envision my Christmas past as something resembling Edmund Gwenn's singing in Dutch to the wide-eyed orphan in the movie. However, in our household, one event was so sour my children used to flee the room when it began: putting up the Christmas tree.

It would always start off hopefully. We would all trek to the neighborhood tree lot, breathing in the pine tree fragrance and selecting the tree. Unfortunately, what looked like the right size at the lot seemed to grow on the way home, leaving me to try to fit a sequoia-sized trunk into a pop bottle–sized tree stand.

At the beginning of this task I would be humming something about Santa Claus coming to town, but soon my mood would degenerate into something that could best be compared to Scrooge being the social director for Mr. Fezziwig's Christmas party.

On one such occasion, after lugging the Shaq-sized pine out to the garage to cut it down to size six times, I finally crammed the tree into the Lilliputian tree stand and began to carve out pieces of the trunk to make the tree appear something other than the Yuletide equivalent of the leaning tower of Pisa. Finally successful, I climbed under the tree for one last adjustment.

That's when the tree fell on me.

Challenged, I leaped up, held the tree at arm's length, and then the unspeakable happened—I punched the family's Christmas tree. Yes, I slugged it right in the trunk, and it went down for the count. Then, I yanked it to its feet, dragged it to the front door, and hurled it onto the lawn. It was the best I felt all evening.

However, when I awoke the next morning, I didn't feel quite so dashing, so I sheepishly snuck out the door to retrieve it before the neighbors could get a glimpse of what goodwill I had toward all men.

Someday, when my children ask about how we celebrated the Yuletide season, I'm sorry, the memory won't be as picturesque as, "Over the river and through the woods, to grandmother's house we go." I'm more mature now. I bought an artificial tree.

I'm Laughing More These Days

Joyce Elsen

I've always worked hard trying to stay fit, through both exercise and sports. I've been playing catch with my granddaughter for years. Last summer she was fifteen years old and playing fast-pitch. After her second throw to me, I walked away and said, "I can't do this anymore. You throw way too hard for me."

Heck, I use to pitch, and now I can barely throw the ball with any speed or distance—underhand. I was still carrying around this little girl not so many years ago. When did this happen?

I never understood why many older women chose to wear pantsuits instead of dresses for special occasions. Now I understand. For some reason, my tennis shoes don't go very well with dresses. I wore heels for an evening a month ago, and the skin is just starting to grow back on those toes.

I used to think my husband and I knew each other so well, we could easily finish each other's sentences. Now I appreciate all those years of practice, because when my girlfriends get together, it takes all of us to complete one person's thought. Thank God we know each other so well. We laugh even more, even if the stories weren't meant to be funny.

Recently my daughter-in-law received a compliment on how beautiful she is, and out of her mouth came, "Oh, thank you so much for saying something. I'm turning forty soon, and you really made me feel good."

Now, when your kids are "feeling their age," you're really old.

I knew I was getting old when my kids were complaining about all their gray hair.

Recently my six-year-old grandchild asked how old I was, and when I answered, she rolled her eyeballs. I noticed I used to be the youngest one at work or on the committee, and now I'm the oldest. I'll hear someone say, "That was back in the seventies, and I wonder why they think that was a long time ago." The worst was when someone said my shoes were squeaky, and I wasn't wearing any.

Thank God for humor, especially during this stage in life. I must admit, I have fun and laugh more often these days, more than any other stage of my adult life.

The Unwanted Harp

BRENDA ELSAGHER

To reduce stress, I began to study the Celtic harp. Anybody can make a harp sound beautiful, and it felt good when I played it. I took lessons from an Irish woman who would encourage me by saying things like, "Everyone has their own pace of learning." I actually think it became her mantra while she worked with me, probably to keep her patience.

I had learned a few Christmas tunes, and it was getting to be that time of the year when I thought I'd entertain my grandmother in the nursing home. She was "safe" for me to perform in front of because she had memory issues, and probably wouldn't be tortured too long remembering my limited performance.

As I began to take the harp out of the bag to carry it in, a woman sitting nearby in a wheelchair started getting irate.

"No, not that! No, take it away."

I started laughing. "Hey, you haven't even heard me play yet."

One of the nearby nurses politely wheeled her away, and my grandma, who then vacillated between decades, enjoyed the music. She couldn't remember my name, and at times, confused me with school girlfriends, but she could sing all the verses of the tunes I played from the Christmas season by memory.

Your Glasses Are on Top of Your Head

We spent an hour singing songs together that afternoon and she didn't tell me to take it away. After I was done playing, she talked to me of her schoolwork she had to do with her girlfriends. The memory of the music might have disappeared for her but not for me. I like to remember her singing verses I'd never heard before and reflect on the peaceful expression on her face as she sang.

Sixty and Shades of Gray

Kathryn Holmes

A dazzling glow peeks through the crevasses of my accordion shades. It reflects like a beacon on my bedroom walls, enticing me to lift my heavy eyelids. No jarring alarm clock to shake my senses. No voice beckoning me to rise and shine. Slowly, I inhale and exhale deeply as I stretch like a cat after an afternoon nap. I relax and contemplate the many ways I am blessed. I can choose to roll over or hop out of bed and start my day. I can choose. After all, I'm retired.

I totter my way out of bed, and for the third and last time, I trot to the Toto. Toto has been my friend since the day she was hooked up and first flipped her lid for me. Actually, Toto is the brand name of the washlet form of toilet. It's like a bidet, only more user-friendly. Toto makes other forms of toilets, but mine is the queen. She lifts the seat when I approach her, sprays warm water on my tush after I've done my business, and then air dries my privates. What a gal!

As I'm brushing my teeth, I happen to notice my hair seems to sparkle from the light above the vanity. A closer look reveals what my beautician told me months ago. It is gray hair. After the highlighted color has been totally snipped off, I can see those strands of gray, and they're spreading. And there seems to be two white patches glaring from each side of my temples. I remember when men who had the same splashes of gray were considered suave, dashing older gentlemen. Not so with women. No longer can I look in disbelief. It's off to call the beauty shop to schedule an appointment. I was born to be a blonde. Why stop now?

Not always have I felt fortunate to have pudgy cheeks. You know, the kind aunts liked to pinch and say, "Ain't she sweet?" Now I'm delighted they puff out my wrinkles, except around my eyes. A little makeup and it's as good as it gets.

I think I'll wear my favorite dusty blue pants with the white flowers today. Who moved the button? Did they shrink? I wonder if I've made too many trips to the snack corner of the kitchen. Chips, you keep tempting me. Now the joke is on me. Wearing my new bra will certainly lift "the girls." Come on, up, up, and away. No! I'm still fighting the thought that I might need a crane and some pulleys to keep them perky. Just don't drag around my waist, please. Waist? Where is it?

One last look in the mirror, and I get my head together. You are a grandmother. You look like a grandmother. Isn't that a joy? And every once in a while, my husband says, "You look cute today." It always surprises me.

Now older, I must admit I regret I never read any of the Dr. Seuss books to my children. Reading some of his quotes today I realize he really was wise. Today, I will be off and running, confident with his telling me, "Today you are You, that is truer than true. There is no one alive who is Youer than You."

Thank you, Dr. Seuss!

ROMEO

Brenda Elsagher

The other day I was getting a massage. My therapist, Terri, said a guy she knew was going out to meet with the other ROMEOs.

My imagination drummed up some young suave guys going out to a bar to pick up women. "Terri, what do you mean? What's a Romeo?"

I cracked up when she told me, "Really Old Men Eating Out."

Growing Older Is Just That—Growing

CHERYL JOBE

I can't remember a time when I didn't have old people in my life. In fact, there have usually been more oldsters than youngsters. Thus, in many ways I looked forward to the aging process.

The elders were fun, and most had an excellent sense of humor, with a much wider view of life in general. You can't have lived all those many years without learning a lot. There were no hang-ups. Will I fit in? What am I going to be when I grow up? Will I marry? If I do, when, to whom? All those big questions plaguing us in our youth had been answered. It had all "come out in the wash," as they say; they knew what was actually needed, and what was fluff and wouldn't matter next week, or in the "big picture."

One friend had a quotation about keeping perspective, which I've clung to these many years since first hearing it: "In a hundred years it won't matter anyway, so why worry over it now?" How many events will be remembered in a hundred years? Surely the momentous events, but never the tears over being stood up for a date, or someone ridiculing a person's sense of style.

Then there are the years when we often feel we are not our own, because being your own person is not always an option. We have a job or career where we must fill a role, children to raise and point in the right direction, a relationship with the spouse to maintain, and other obligations, not always in this order. When there is time to spare for a hobby or relaxing on our own, however brief, is when we can connect with the "me" inside. It's not unusual to lose touch with ourselves, disembodied in a way, like forgetting an old friend, either the name or the face.

Being somewhat artistic and creative in nature, and to be quite honest, more than a little eccentric, age has allowed me to drop the conventions that bind. Elders have the freedom to laugh at those things that aren't funny to anyone else, to tell mildly inappropriate jokes that make children giggle and their parents roll their eyes.

We can see styles and modes repeat themselves and not get caught up in them. When I see the young girls with their hair dyed blue or purple or a garish red, it reminds me of my grandmother. For special occasions, she and her friends went rather wild. Before the curlers were placed strategically to cover thinning spots, a pale blue or lavender or pink rinse might be applied to their silver or white hair.

I came from the generation of women who shunned girdles and often bras. Curlers were a non-thing, as was makeup for many. While seeing lipstick and foundation as artificial, akin to wearing a mask, most of us clung to our black eyeliner and mascara. Looking at old photos, I realize I wasn't bad-looking back then with makeup on, but I wouldn't look anything like that now. As for hair, the long locks of my yesterday are gone, kept short enough so I no longer think I really should do something with it, even though those thoughts were fleeting.

Your Glasses Are on Top of Your Head

My wardrobe varies from bright and vivid colors, which reflect the artist in me, to faded, stained, and ragged. Long skirts or jeans cover up the spider veins, or the fact I gave up razors years ago because shaving irritated my skin. My clothing reflects who I am, not an indicator of a job or position in life, all with no pretensions. I like this thought: one's appearance should be a verb, and not a noun. I may be a no-body, but I'm some-body and not some-thing. This is comfortable, earned, and to be cherished.

When talking with a friend recently, we discussed the fact that thanks to computers, music of every genre has lost its texture. From Maybelle Carter to Jimi Hendrix there were guts, grit, grain, and feel to music—satin and cotton, burlap and velvet. Elders are the keepers of the best and worst of "what used to be." Crazy old lady, or woman of acquired wisdom, depending on one's outlook, and I'm proud to be a part of it. How else will those who come after us know the taste of food that didn't come from a box, a can, or out of a microwave, or know the difference between an icebox and a refrigerator, a privy and a port-a-potty?

Growing older is just that—growing. We hold the keys from the past to the future so humanity can continue in a long, seamless flow. My grandfather taught me that one should never stop learning, whether it is a new fact, or a new word, or meeting a new person. Because, he said, when you stop learning is when you begin to die within yourself.

I like myself better now than when I was young. One gets to a point where she is comfortable in her own skin, after all. By now her skin is a bit baggy, a little frayed, and has had some repairs. We're much like a comfy pair of shoes you don't wear in public but can't bear to part with. We are now the culmination of our life's experiences, which I prefer to call the grand finale.

Settled now, I live on a raw piece of hillside with my dear husband of forty-two years, three dogs, and a horse. The long years of being town-bound are over, and I am content.

Don't wait for your dreams to become reality. Chase them down and tackle them.

The Inspirational Wrinkle

BRENDA ELSAGHER

I had prepared for my talk to telephone qualifiers for a market research company. I took them back to my younger years when I worked in the same position. We had a lot of laughs, and I shared some of the challenges I faced over the years, and how my early work in the research company served me in every job I ever had.

My goal was to affirm them in their career choices, remind them they are the smile and introduction to the company they work for, and they create a very important first impression. I wanted to emphasize that their jobs were valuable and important. The thirty minutes flew by, and I thought it went well, judging by their applause and their enthusiasm, plus the owners were very pleased.

As a bonus gift, I handed each a copy of my first book, and in doing so, I shook each person's hand before they returned to work. One woman hung back from the rest. Usually when people wait around, I know they want to share a personal story with me.

"You really inspired me, Brenda!" Inside I beamed. I am happy I did what I wanted to achieve, I thought to myself. Then she continued.

"For a long time, I've been trying to cover up the wrinkle in the middle of my forehead; you know, the one appearing when you squint your eyes in the sun? See mine? I've been covering it up with my bangs for years. You inspired me because I see you have a big one too, and you don't even try to cover it up. I am wearing mine proudly from now on."

I guess inspiration isn't always what you'd predict. I'm glad I inspired her. She inspired me too in the opposite manner. I'm thinking of getting some cosmetic "help" now.

Tracker Panic

NOREEN BRAMAN

This morning I wore my electronic fitness tracker on my wrist, still in the nighttime wristband, while I cleaned the bathroom and put away laundry.

I was suddenly distracted by a medical emergency with Dewey, my cockatiel, who was covered with blood. I whisked her to the sink to clean her up, and found no active bleeding, just a lot of feathers coming in. I guess she pulled on one, or got it caught somehow. I bathed her, cuddled her in a towel, then returned her to her cage under a warm light bulb to help her dry and feel better. I gave a sigh of relief as she began preening herself, chirping, and eating. Whew, how scary.

Then I realized I was no longer wearing my electronic fitness tracker. I assumed I had taken it off before bathing my bird, but it wasn't near the sink, the towels, or Dewey's cage. Then I thought maybe I took it off while cleaning the bathroom. It wasn't in there either. I started to feel annoyed and upset with myself. Lately I'd been forgetting where I put down my cell phone, and have had to go back to my bathroom in the morning to make sure the curling iron was turned off.

Short-term memory loss, I thought. Now it begins. My concern turned into panic. No, no, this can't be happening. I have way too much left to do in my life. My grandchildren are only babies. It took me fifty years to find the Love of My Life (LOML). I left the house to run an errand, and drove through the nearby park, taking in the brilliant fall colors just to calm myself.

When I got home, the LOML braved both the kitchen and bathroom garbage cans. No tracker. The darn thing was still synching to my phone, so we knew it was in the house. But where in the world did I put it? The freezer? Isn't it a typical hiding place for those with memory problems to put things? Not there. Not in the laundry, or the dog's dish, or my shoes. Nor was it pushed under the couch or the dresser by the vacuum today.

Finally, I looked up some helpful hints for finding a lost electronic fitness tracker. Yes, the manufacturer actually has such a webpage. Most of the usual places I had already checked. And yes, it was still synching, so it had to be in the house.

The final hint was to download a Bluetooth device locator onto my phone. Well, not an actual locator, but a meter telling you which Bluetooth devices are communicating with your phone, and their signal strength. I loaded the software and turned on my laptop. It showed up right away, with a strong signal. Then, there was my tracker, a weak signal, but there.

As I walked away from the computer, the signal weakened, but the tracker's got stronger. As I walked farther away from the computer, the tracker got stronger and stronger, until I was standing in front of my closet, the same closet where I had placed freshly laundered clothes a few hours earlier. Ah-ha!

The hunt wasn't as easy as I expected. The tracker and its wristband were not just lying on the closet floor. In fact, the signal at the floor was weaker. Above the closet pole it was also weaker. Apparently the tracker was somewhere in the clothes. Eventually, I had to go through a bunch of items where the signal was the strongest, and there it was, my black wristband, securely fastened to the sleeve of a black shirt by the famous hook-and-loop fastener designed to keep it around my wrist. Apparently my tracker had jumped ship, attached itself to the nearest arm, and hung there, like a bat, snoozing.

My relief was twofold. First, I was happy to find this expensive electronic gadget. Second, I realized this was just "one of those things" on "one of those days," and it had nothing to do with memory loss, short term or otherwise. In fact, I think I burned some new neural pathways playing detective and utilizing some new software.

But perhaps the most important thing I learned was that someone loves me enough to dump out two cans of smelly garbage to look for something we both thought I had mindlessly misplaced. And you can't complain about such a delightful act of kindness.

Senior Citizen Discount

Brenda Elsagher

Recently I met my friend Monica at the theater. We got to our seats a few minutes early before the movie started and began to chat.

Suddenly she said, "I just realized I could have gotten the senior discount since I just had my sixtieth birthday two weeks ago!"

"How much is a discounted ticket?"

"The tickets are usually $10.00 but with a senior discount, they are only $7.50."

We laughed for a second before I realized I had received the discounted price.

"I paid $7.50. The cashier never asked how old I was, and I won't be a senior for a couple more years."

Monica told me she felt better.

Upper Structure

Barbara Kelley Linkous

When our daughter Georga, named after her daddy, George, was born, I was determined to breastfeed her. Contrary to my desire, I was not having much success. A nurse came into my hospital room one day, and scared the heck out of me with a suction-cup-looking gizmo. She said curtly, "We are going to learn how to breastfeed your daughter." Luckily for me, someone had the ingenuity to invent baby bottles.

When Georga was about six years old, she inquired, "What are those things?"

I referred to them as my "upper structure" (my breasts). Those are rather big words for such a little tyke, but she seemed satisfied with my answer. As I grew older, my "upper structure" began to droop, clean into my drawers. Because I have scoliosis of the back, my "upper structure" sagged even more than the norm. The song, "Do Your Ears Hang Low?" kept going through my mind. Not my ears, but something else, I thought.

Because of my back, I felt my "upper structure" was too heavy and could be causing my back to curve more. I decided I would have a mastectomy. I soon visited a boob specialist who said they were too small, and besides, Medicare would not pay for the procedure, to which I loudly retorted, "What do you mean too small? It has taken me thirty years to get them this size!"

I was devastated, because ever since high school, I had tried every means available to reach my goal. I applied cocoa butter to them, and I even sent away to a mail order company, which guaranteed its product to increase the size of my upper structure. They sent a fabric hand. The instructions indicated I was to massage the area until desired size was reached. I never did try the ridiculous apparatus.

One day I overheard a conversation between Georga and one of her second-grade classmates about my "upper structure."

The classmate said, "Those aren't called 'upper structure.' They're breasts."

Georga responded, "My mother told me that's what they're called, and she's always right." Because Georga's classmates were so "sharp," I was always getting caught if I did not say the exact word. From then on, I referred to my "upper structure" as my breasts.

Today I'm eighty-one years old. My "upper structure" still hangs low and I wish I could swing them right out the window. What I once needed for Georga as a baby is an integral part of me, and all these years later, it's a wonderful reminder of the love of our beautiful baby girl in my arms.

Life Is Sweet

Mary Drago

In our living room, we have a picture of my husband and me on our wedding day. Oh, we were so young! At age twenty-two, I was beautiful, slim, and had clear skin and lustrous, long dark hair. These days, as I look in the mirror, the skin is older, the circles under the eyes more pronounced, the thin hair needs more touch-ups. I can't even put a bobby pin in it anymore. Odd little hairs are sprouting on my chin like a newly fertilized garden. The knees are stiffer. And I live in my glasses. Not only have I looked for them when they were on top of my head, I've even looked for them when I've been wearing them. I have multiple pairs stashed around the house and in my purse. And most annoying is falling asleep at 7 p.m. while wearing them and then rolling over on the darned things, which causes the wire ones to bend, and the plastic ones to break.

While my mother was in home hospice as I cared for her, she used to say, "Life is sweet." Yes it is, even with all the hard-earned lumps and bumps, creaky knees, and extra weight, for they are a badge of life. Life is sweet, and to be treasured, and I plan to keep laughing through it as long and hard as I can. Even the Bible says there is a time to laugh—and this is it.

With my husband beside me, I look at my older self, and we laughingly joke about what we want to be dressed in for our

39

final journey. Perhaps something elegant, or maybe our paisley jacket and velvet pants, or a long dress? Or should I just wear a favorite T-shirt my husband bought as a gag gift printed with, "The Sarcasm Is Strong in This One!" complimented by sweat pants, sunglasses, and my favorite purse or two?

Jokingly, I've often told my husband he can lay me out in my wedding gown, slit up the back, of course, to fit. He sarcastically informs me the casket next to me is going to hold my shoes, purses, china, bric-a-brac, and clothes I have collected over the years, and now am loathe to part with because they will come back in style. What does it matter if my closet holds size 8 to XXL?

In my mother's final journey in 2001 of breast cancer, she had a little plaid suitcase in a bedroom closet packed with what she wanted to be buried in: the suit she wore at my wedding, a new bra, a new slip, and pretty shoes. I laughed when I saw the pair of "Never Run Panty Hose" that she must have purchased around 1969 from a drugstore for the princely sum of $1.99, with the tag still on the unopened package. I used to tease her that she couldn't meet God with a run in her hose.

She was such a planner, complete with a bank account opened for the occasion of her death to be spent on the burial plot, the funeral home, and the luncheon in the church hall after the burial, so "we didn't have to worry about a thing."

So here we are, my husband and I, taking a page out of Mom's book. Life is sweet, and it is good to laugh through it.

The Joys of Growing Older

Roberta Gold

I was prepared, had rehearsed, dressed professionally, and was ready. Walking into the room, the audience was already seated—backs to me, lights off except for the stage. I waited until I was introduced before I started the final stroll. As I turned to look at the audience, they all gave me a standing ovation welcome. Just as I was about to break into my opening monologue, the lights went on brightly, and I was staring into the eyes of all my friends and family as they yelled, "Surprise!" and began singing "Happy Birthday" to me. What a way to celebrate my thirtieth birthday.

Birthdays have always been special in my family. What child wasn't eager to turn sixteen and be able to drive? Then it was turning eighteen, and becoming legal at twenty-one, a milestone we all looked forward to reaching. Mine was quite memorable. My mother, brother, sister-in-law, grandparents, and best friend all came over to celebrate. My father was very sick, and stayed in his bedroom.

We were all sitting around the kitchen table when my grandfather asked my mother if those were marijuana cigarettes sitting in the ashtrays around the table.

"The doctor thought it would help with the nausea. Do you want to try one?" she asked.

We were soon passing the joint around the table.

My grandmother looked upset, and we asked her if she was all right.

"Well, no one passed it to me!"

We couldn't stop laughing.

Most birthdays usually involved a great meal and a wonderful cake, so this was a bonus.

I have always celebrated with wild abandon: skydiving, a hot air balloon ride, a canoe trip, a casino night, or just letting loose and dancing the night away.

Yet, as time goes on, more is happening than adding another year to my life. Why do I see my mother's face when I look in the mirror? Why doesn't my body bend the way it used to? I feel a freedom since I don't care what anyone thinks anymore. I realize as I get older, there are definite benefits of attitude. I am not terrified to go outside without makeup. I am not trying to impress anyone but myself. I am not as judgmental about how my body looks. I have more of a "Who cares?" attitude now. I realize I can relax and simply enjoy everything around me.

You see, it isn't about being skinny anymore. I am grateful I can take a walk every morning, and watch the sun bring a spectacular glowing start to the day. Watching a friend recover from a serious accident helps me face obstacles in my own life.

After living in a large ranch-style house with a yard, pool, and hillside for the past twenty years, moving to a one-bedroom apartment is easier when I reframe it and view it as a huge, beautiful hotel with amenities all taken care of by someone else.

Having a positive attitude is effortless when you let go of the stuff that brought you down. I think birthdays are great "inventory" days—a time to look back with relief and ahead with excitement. A new year begins, and you can start fresh.

Your Glasses Are on Top of Your Head

All the projects where I overestimated my abilities can begin again, or I am able to change them to better reign in my expectations so I can realistically finish what I set out to accomplish. It doesn't matter where I go, it matters more who I am with, and how much fun we are having. I can change my attitude easier, look at things from the other side, give the benefit of the doubt, turn the other cheek, and find the humor in the situation.

Getting older means I can relax and enjoy life to the fullest. I am looking forward to all the new adventures waiting for me.

One-Handed Humor

RUTH BACHMAN

Statistics tell us one in two men, and one in three women, will be diagnosed with cancer in their lifetime. Statistics also tell us the majority of those diagnoses will be made in individuals who are sixty-five or older. While very little is funny about a cancer diagnosis, a sense of humor will help in navigating the journey.

In 2003, I was a wife and mother in apparent good health. A small, non-painful lump on the inside of my left wrist turned out to be a six-inch mass, beginning in my hand, filling my wrist, and extending into my forearm. A biopsy brought the diagnosis of very high-grade Malignant Fibrous Histiocytoma, the most common form of soft-tissue sarcoma, a very uncommon form of cancer.

Learning that the acceptable margin for resection was 2.5 centimeters, 1-inch all around, and knowing that my wrist was full, I cut to the chase. My doctor affirmed my assumption: the best treatment outcome would involve the amputation of my dominant left hand. Having been a left-handed woman for fifty-four years, I had grown rather attached to that hand.

My first response was fear. How was I going to button my jeans? Write my name? Put on makeup? Cut my meat? Peel a carrot? Make French braids in a little girl's hair? My mind was racing with questions. My faith was the antidote to my fear. My heart knew I would make the transition to accepting the inevitable and move forward, which I did. I spent the next three months in active cancer treatment, including chemo, working with occupational therapists to learn to be one-handed and right handed. I lost my hair before losing my hand, and having my husband tie scarves on my bald head after surgery was laughable at times.

Since losing my hand to cancer, I am regularly confronted with things that appear to be two-handed. On those occasions, I learn to do something a new way, ask for help, or decide not to do that thing—and I have rarely chosen the third option. Not only have I learned to be fiercely independent in my one-handedness, I have also learned that asking someone to help, allowing someone to help, is a gift to them as well as a gift to me. From sliding suitcases into an overhead compartment on an airplane to peeling and dicing potatoes, I have found help in creativity, gadgets, and the kindness of strangers to assist me in making it through the day.

Ten months after my amputation, I became a grandmother to a very special little girl. I was shopping for a cute spring holiday outfit in the children's department while I was wearing a new wool winter jacket. I live in Minnesota, so wearing a winter jacket, purchased at end-of-season sale price, while shopping for a spring outfit is not so unusual.

Often pockets of a new garment are sewn closed, awaiting the new owner to split the stitches and open them for use. My jacket was one of those because I had not yet opened it. I walked through the store as I fidgeted with my right fingers to loosen the threads of the sewn right pocket. It was simply something to do while I shopped. I worked intently until I could relatively easily slip my hand into the opening, planning to expand the remaining threads and open the remainder of the enclosure. My plan became flawed when I realized not only did I not have enough leverage to open the remaining stitches, but my hand became securely entrapped in the partially opened pocket.

As I entered the children's department, I laughed to myself as I struggled to free my hand. I knew I could have taken off the jacket and freed my hand, but I decided to choose another option.

A salesperson approached me and said, "May I help you with something?"

I smiled and replied, "Yes, but it is probably not what you think it might be. Would you help me get my hand out of my pocket?"

The woman looked at me with skepticism and concern. Only when I displayed my remaining left limb, missing what certainly would have been a helpful hand, did she begin to comprehend what I needed her to do. I explained the situation, and with a huge, helpful smile, she extracted my right hand from the partially opened pocket, and we went on together to find a suitable and adorable outfit for my granddaughter.

I have witnessed the kindness of strangers firsthand many times as a cancer survivor; being surrounded by a community of support helps through the cancer journey. A few perks come along with amputation, thanks to a dear friend who pointed out positive aspects of amputation in an email sent before my surgery.

I have half as many age spots as other women my age. I have the opportunity to seek half-priced manicures. I will never again lose a pair of gloves. And I know the sound of one hand clapping.

Maintaining my sense of humor during times of challenge is an important key to resilience. It is what has helped me accept trials without being totally overwhelmed by them, at least not for too long . . .

I wish the same for you.

Minnesota Interesting

Brenda Elsagher

My husband is not a slave to fashion. He boasts that he's kept certain trends alive for twenty-five years. We're talking white shoes with two-inch heels, which he wore beyond the era they were popular. I am thankful that because he is from Egypt, he didn't know about the matching white belt that accessorized the shoes, and apparently no one informed him it was unfashionable to wear white after Labor Day.

Christmas Eve night attending midnight mass with my family, only one month after we were married, he wore the white shoes for that special occasion. He had polished them many times over, and they looked it. People teased *me* all the time about *his* shoes. Even after I thought I convinced him to reconsider that choice, he'd wear those shoes. I told him they were not flattering, but Bahgat never lacked self-confidence.

Another time, much to his delight, his brother sent him cream-colored patent leather shoes from Egypt—of course with two-inch heels. He loved them. By this time he was a manager at a big technology firm. Sensing he wanted to wear them to work, I discouraged him.

"Bahgat, those shoes are not stylish, and people notice things like that."

I bought him nice leather loafers, but he was not interested in them.

One day he came home from work and when I was hugging him, I glanced at his feet.

"What's with those shoes you're wearing?" Wherever there was a crease from where he bent his foot, white showed through on otherwise black shoes.

And then it hit me. "Oh. My. God. Bahgat, you didn't spray paint your cream shoes from Egypt, did you?"

He smiled as he said, "Brenda, I want you to know that all day long people were complimenting me on them."

Horrified, I asked, "What exactly did they say?"

"Very interesting shoes," he happily reported. "You wouldn't believe all the comments on them, people thought they were great."

"Bahgat, in Minnesota, when people tell you 'That's interesting,' it's not usually good. In Minnesota-nice language it really means, 'Someone should tell that poor soul to get a clue, *but it's not going to be me.*'"

Months before, we had seen a four-foot-tall windmill in a neighbor's yard that had little boxes on the bottom for flowers. I had stopped and admired it, and the man told us how long it took him to make it. He thought of selling them for $300. It was just small talk. When we walked away, I commented on how cute it was, and Bahgat relayed he would never want one of those things in his yard.

Maybe if I was twenty years older, I would not have cared what people thought of his shoes, but I wasn't there yet. I hoped we had a long life ahead of us even though I could clearly see I had little influence over him. Not much has changed.

This latest shoe action made me resort to threats.

"Bahgat, if you ever wear those shoes again, I am going to buy that windmill and put it in our front yard for everyone to see. I might even buy two."

Luckily for both of us, he never wore them again.

Section II
Memory Lapse Follies

Overheard: A woman at work was looking all over for her reader glasses. Finally, I couldn't stand it any longer. "Just curious, would those work? You know, the ones on top of your head?"

—Anonymous

Good Vibrations

Jeanette Kane

Last summer, I had lunch with my friends Dolly and Ed and planned to go see a fun play immediately afterwards called *The Church Basement Ladies*. We are dear friends, and I've known Dolly for twenty-eight years through line dancing. We always have fun together, and still had more excitement planned for later in the evening. Our next event was to see one of my favorite shows about Elvis Presley, and we agreed to all go home and get refreshed for an hour before heading out again. I was excited to see the show, and very conscious of the little time I had before they would pick me up. Aware Ed is a stickler on time, and that I didn't want to keep him waiting, I hurried along.

Right when I was walking up to my door I noticed my flowers were wilted and drooping, in need of a drink. It was a warm day, and I got the hose out and quickly watered them right away. When I was done taking care of the garden, I headed in to change clothes, now worrying about how much time I spent in the garden and trying not to be late for Ed, who would be picking me up soon.

Then I realized, oh gosh, I still have to change my clothes. I was still outside when I realized in my hurrying, I had mis-placed my cell phone. I looked all through my purse, then I retraced my steps and looked everywhere I walked, thinking

I must have dropped it on the ground. After getting more frantic searching the garden, I couldn't figure out where I had put it.

I concluded it must be in their car because I was with them most of the day. Getting short on time, I called Dolly and explained my predicament.

"I think I must have dropped my phone in the back seat of your car."

This prompted them to make a thorough search, scouring every square inch before Ed called me back, offering, "I'll dial your phone number, and see if you can hear it anywhere. Hopefully, it's nearby."

When he called me, very soon I felt a vibration between my plentiful breasts. I started laughing as I thought back to how it had probably happened when I had to stuff my phone somewhere when I reached for the hose. We all got a huge laugh out of it, and I told the story the following week at line dancing. One lady said it would never happen to her because she was too flat and it would fall right out. Then we all had another good laugh.

RE: Lost Billfold

KATHRYN HAMMER

An actual email exchange between sisters:

To: Kathy
From: Molly

If Bob found the frozen blueberries in the junk drawer, where do you think I'd put my billfold?

To: Molly
From: Kathy

Re: Frozen blue billfold.

Assuming you've determined to a degree of confidence that the billfold wasn't stolen or left someplace while you were out, it's likely in the house or garage. The key is to retrace your steps (obvious), while retracing the details of what you were doing and thinking about at the time. (Not so obvious and possibly scary.)

Here, let me help with some possible scenarios . . .

You were on the phone while walking around and tidying up. You were carrying a laundry basket, throwing stray things in on top of the clothes to go upstairs, including your billfold, which wasn't in your purse because you'd taken it out earlier in the morning to give Alex a credit card you'd loaded for him yesterday. You spotted your robe slung over the banister, so you threw it on top of the stuff in the basket. Obviously, the billfold will be found in the basket as soon as you get around to sorting the clean socks. Except, it won't be. It will be in your robe pocket, because you were wearing it when you gave Alex the credit card before you had your coffee.

You were in the car at a stoplight, rifling through your purse for something. You removed the wallet for roomier, more efficient rummaging, and set it next to you. The car behind you honked for you to get a move on, you ditzy woman, so you momentarily postponed putting the wallet back in the purse and it slipped between the seats. "Momentarily" turned into a chronic condition.

You were making a utility payment over the phone and took the wallet out of your purse to get the debit card. But suddenly you had to go to the bathroom and ran in there, wallet in hand, which you tossed into the magazine box alongside the toilet because you needed both hands to get your pants down. And, because the doorbell rang just as you were finishing, you had to hurry, hurry, hurry, and promptly forgot about the wallet.

You were juggling groceries from the car, and your purse kept slipping off your shoulder, so as you were opening the door into the house, you just let it slide to the floor/step at the entry, with the intent of retrieving it when your hands were free—which you did. But you didn't notice the purse had tipped over, dumping the billfold, which is now next to the refrigerator in the garage . . . which is also where you'll find your lipstick, $1.13 in change, and a half tin of breath mints.

You were walking around while on the phone and, spying the wallet lying on the kitchen table, you picked it up, intending to put it back in your purse. But then your dog started whining to go outside, so you took the opportunity to step out and retrieve the dead plant you'd set out there last fall. But then your dog demanded you throw the ball, so to keep him quiet (because you're on the phone) you do so, but first you have to set the wallet down on the grill in order to free up a hand, which is where it now is, assuming the raccoons living in the woodpile haven't run off with it.

Or it's on a dining room/kitchen chair seat pushed nicely into place at the table. You've walked by it a hundred times without seeing it.

Oh, I don't know. I made up all those things because I really don't have any experience with misplacing things . . .

Kind regards,

Your older yet mentally intact sister

Epilogue: The billfold was eventually located at the cell phone service provider's store. When asked why they didn't call Molly to say they had the billfold, they responded, "We didn't have your number." Everyone who works there is under thirty.

You Were the Easiest

MARY KAY MORRISON

It has been my routine to call my ninety-two-year-old mother several times a week. She lives in a retirement home about three hours from me. It was difficult when she was diagnosed with Alzheimer's several years ago, since my father died of this terrible disease in 1997. I am the oldest of seven siblings, but most have moved to other parts of the country and are unable to travel to see Mom as often as they would like. It is fortunate I am able to travel to see her several times a month. When we are together, we frequently tease about which sibling "she likes best." One of our family's favorite ways to tease the others is to say, "Mom always liked you best."

Recently I have felt apprehensive when I call Mom, wondering how long it will be before she no longer recognizes my voice. However, she always sounds happy to hear from me, and says, "Hi, Mary Kay." Last week when I called we chatted for a while, and I told her about one of our nieces having a baby. Of course we were both delighted to welcome a new little one into our large family.

Mom then said, "You were the easiest."

Of course, I was quite happy to hear this, and repeated, "I was the easiest child?"

She affirmed I was absolutely the easiest. I was secretly

thinking it would be great fun to brag to my siblings about what Mom had said about me being the easiest child. I had visions of immediately calling them to let them know I was indeed the best baby and easiest child in the family.

As I was planning a strategy to convey to the siblings my mother's affirmation that I was the most angelic child, my mother decisively said, "Yes, Mary Kay was the hardest!"

Unstylish Shoes

Bev Biller

I recently returned to my job at a large teaching hospital after my second knee replacement. As the Wound, Ostomy Continence nurse there, one of my responsibilities is coordinating the quarterly Prevalence Study in which all patients, potentially three hundred, have total skin assessments to look for any pressure ulcers. Prevalence Day is always a non-stop, busy day, and the next day invariably my office is swamped with consults for new patients to follow.

It was late in the day after my first Prevalence Study since my return from my medical leave. I had sought haven in my office for an opportunity to kick my shoes under my desk and enjoy a quick bite to eat. After my allotted half hour, I slipped back into my shoes, and off I went again. As I walked the distance back to the hospital's main building, I began thinking of my new knees and how, after these two very busy days, they didn't feel quite right. It felt like my legs were a little uneven. I worried the stress of the last days had revealed a major problem.

I got into the elevator to head up to my next patient, leaned against the back wall, and turned my gaze toward the floor. Then I noticed at the end of my black-stockinged feet were a black rubber clog on the left and a stylish black flat on the right.

Relief, but embarrassment. With my day quickly coming to a close, I had no time to return to my office to find the proper mate to one of my shoes. I suffered through the remaining hour and a half with my unstylish look, and was able to bring a bit of comic relief to many nurses.

That's Amazing!

Brenda Elsagher

For months I was eating healthier and losing weight. Even though I had lost seventy pounds, I still had much to lose, so most people didn't notice. I hadn't talked about it much because I usually found the weight back on again in a matter of time, so I was trying to keep it on the down low.

One afternoon I was visiting with my mother who struggled with dementia. My siblings and I helped out quite a bit because Dad had some health issues and was in transitional care for a while. I was on the Sunday/Monday shift and had Mom all to myself, which was rarely the case with seven siblings competing for her attention.

Growing up with my mom, there was never a doubt that she loved me, but she was tough at times. A former high-level administrative assistant, parish council president, and mother of eight, she was a no-nonsense woman. A hard worker, with many talents as a gourmet cook and delicious bread maker, she could also have a tough exterior.

I wouldn't describe her as the cookies-and-milk kind of mother, who'd ever say, "Here, honey, sit down and tell me about your day, and enjoy some warm chocolate chip cookies fresh out of the oven."

No, more like, "You made your bed, you lie on it."

You could always count on her for an honest opinion, whether you asked for it or not. She was a straight shooter with too many responsibilities and too little time, and no doubt she did the best she could.

These days, the dementia brought out a very pleasant side of her, and she was content in life. She was sweet, complimentary, always enjoyed my jokes, and we loved to hear her laugh at them even though she'd heard them many times before. We could easily redirect her thinking and attitude by the one we reflected toward her. We were lucky; sometimes with dementia, it doesn't end up that way. I relaxed around her and enjoyed the moments with her, knowing they would be gone from her memory shortly after. She loved symphonies and plays, but as we walked out of the building, she may have already forgotten what she just saw or heard. She loved soft things and became soft herself, but she wasn't before she started losing her short-term memory.

So on this lovely afternoon I confessed quietly, "Mom, guess what? I've lost seventy pounds."

"Wow, that's amazing. I'm so proud of you!"

Well, not one to hear many compliments from my mom over the years, I relished in it. So about ten minutes later, I said, "Hey, Mom, guess what? I've lost seventy pounds."

"Wow, that's amazing. I'm so proud of you!"

It felt so good to hear those words from her, I enjoyed it for about ten more minutes. I could not help myself when I told her one more time, "Mom, guess what? I've lost seventy pounds!"

She delivered her same response as enthusiastically as the other two times. "Wow, that's amazing. I'm so proud of you!" Finally, I guess I was filled up with compliments.

Several months later, on my Sunday/Monday shift, I

recalled our earlier conversation and had more to report, wondering if history would repeat itself. So I tried it out, this time with news she hadn't heard.

"Mom, guess what? I've lost a hundred pounds."

"Wow, that's amazing. I'm so proud of you, but you must have really been out of control!"

Ah, the old mother was back just for a moment, and I kind of enjoyed it.

Hurrying to My Cousin

MARILYN SPEIKER

Years ago, I went to work extra early at 4 a.m. at my job for the city so I could get off by 10 a.m. with plans to bring my cousin to her appointment. She had lost her arm in a farming accident, and I was going to bring her to see a prosthetic specialist.

I had been hurrying all morning, trying to get everything done before work. Then I raced through work, and got on the road to get to the appointment for my cousin thirty miles away. That was thirty-five years ago when my cousin had the accident. It seems like only yesterday and these days I'm seventy-four years old. Now I can legitimately use age as my reason for losing things. Now, I've lost my place in the dance line, I've lost how to get to my own place (even in my younger years), and I've lost my place in a book.

On the day I was to pick up my cousin, I was halfway to where she had her appointment when I realized something: I had lost my mind for a few minutes and had forgotten my cousin and had to go back to get her. She's the only one who can legitimately say she lost something—which was her arm!

The Scare of Losing My Phone

KAREL MURRAY

While waiting for my flight in the Chicago O'Hare airport, I decided to call a business associate on my mobile phone to discuss a new program I was designing. Seated at a table, I was surrounded by other travelers who were also enjoying their lunch. About halfway through the call, my business associate wanted the address of a mutual friend.

"Let me find my cell phone and I'll look it up."

Before he could speak, I placed my iPhone face down on the table and began to look through my purse to find my cell phone. Digging aggressively through the bag, I discovered it wasn't in my purse.

With a bit of panic, I picked up my phone and said to my associate, "Just a minute . . . I can't seem to find my cell phone. I'll be right back."

I put my cell phone back down on the table and began to search through my laptop bag. Still no phone. By this time, sheer desperation took over because this phone held all of my contact and travel information, and it was vital I didn't lose it.

I turned to a young couple about four feet away and announced, "I can't find my phone. Have you seen it anywhere? Did I drop it on the floor or something? Please help!"

With a look of pity reserved only for those who seem

to have lost all of their senses, he simply pointed at my cell phone on the table and said, "You've been talking on it."

Huh.

With a smile of absolute gratitude, I seized up the phone and said, "Why didn't you tell me I was already talking on the phone and was holding it in my hand the entire time?"

He laughed so loud he had a small problem with catching his breath. He was just going to wait to see how long it took me to realize I was already on the phone when I went to search for the phone.

I think I need one of those strings they use to attach to mittens as a small child and put one on my phone. At least I'll know it's close by, and I can just tug on the string and bring it back into my hands.

On the Tip of My Tongue

LINDA O'CONNELL

"You know what's-her-name?" I ask my husband.

"Who? What is her name?" he asks, knowing full well if I could pull up her name, I'd have done so.

"Oh, you know who I mean, the gal with short hair."

"A lot of women fit the description." He hounds me like a detective. "More details. What's her name?"

I glare at him, hold up my index finger. In my mind, I start at letter A and go all the way to letter Z. I try to identify the first letter in her name, hoping it will jump out and magically collect the rest of the letters, spell it out like those plastic ABCs on the side of the fridge. I can't retrieve the information, at least not at the moment. If I give it a while, quite a while, suddenly and unexpectedly, when I am paying the cashier at the grocery store, or out to dinner with a friend, I'll spurt the name right off the tip of my tongue where it's been hovering for the last twenty-four to thirty-six hours. The unknowing young cashier won't figure out why I called her the wrong name. She'll point to her name badge, and introduce herself as though she thinks I am illiterate.

Once I was at a restaurant when I spouted the wrong name because I now remembered the right one. The college-age waiter repeated her name slowly and concisely. No reason to explain; nobody ever believes forgetfulness will happen to them. Smile and nod, which I do a lot these days.

The conversation between my husband and me is as goofy as the Abbott and Costello episode. After a while, neither of us sees the humor in it. It's bad enough he has moderate hearing loss, due to years of working around noisy machinery. He thinks I say one thing when I actually say another, and I swear, he does it on purpose because he can definitely hear my muttering from another room, but not my sentences when we're sitting in the living room just a few feet apart. The hearing loss, coupled with the age-related memory loss of two over-sixty-year-olds, sometimes can make a day unbearable. I've begun using sign language, not the official American Sign Language, just hand motions to get my point across.

"Do you want to get something to eat?" I ask.

He looks at my shoes and empathetically asks, "What's wrong with your feet?"

I pretend I'm shoveling food in my open mouth and say, "Eat, eat!"

"Are you hungry?" he asks.

"What do you want?" I ask.

He repeats, "What do you want?"

I know he hears every word I say.

When I told him recently we had a fundraising event for my school, he moaned.

"Not only can't I hear well, but I can't remember names anymore," he complained. "You're going to have to be the ears and brains if we go."

"No problem," I assured him. I had heard a memory expert on TV explain how to remember a list, saying, "For example, if you need bread, eggs, milk, and shampoo, you can memorize the first letter of each word. BEMS would be an acronym for those items." My husband reminded me he's dyslexic.

"If all else fails, you can use visualization techniques to get the feel of the objects by engaging your five senses. For instance, to remember things, imagine sticking the items onto yourself. Imagine a loaf of bread under your shirt on your stomach near your 'bread basket.' Then, imagine balancing each of the eggs on your arms without dropping them. Put the milk on your knee, and imagine the weight of it as you walk. Last, visualize the entire bottle of shampoo drizzling over your head."

"What are you implying about my stomach?" he asked. I smiled. He balked, "If I imagined a dozen eggs rolling up and down my arms, I'd begin to act ridiculous. Don't you think people would stare if I started dragging one leg, wiping my eyes while flapping my arms? Not to mention trying not to smash my gut, I mean the bread."

"But don't you think this is a good technique, and it could potentially work if you didn't act it out, and just thought it out?" I pressured him. He agreed this could work for some, if the list were short.

"So, at the event, when I introduce you to someone, I want you to say their name out loud as you greet the person, and then touch a body part and make the name stick. Will you at least try?" He agreed. At the event, dressed in our finest, I introduced my husband to coworkers. He greeted the person by name, and then rubbed his elbow, shrugged, or patted his thigh. I winked my approval. As the evening wore on, I asked how he was doing.

"I can't remember if it's your boss or her husband who's in my pocket, and I'm going to look spastic if I start smacking myself around every time someone comes over to talk."

I offered my assistance and assurance. "I'll stay close to you since the names aren't sticking." A couple whose children I had taught approached. I tried to introduce them to my husband. I said, "Honey this is . . ."

Nothing! My mind went blank. I could not remember their names. However, I could retrieve needless details about them: where they lived, what their occupations were, their jogging routes, but not one of their names. I smiled, tried to save the moment.

I turned away from the couple, and with a Vanna White hand sweep, said, "This is my husband."

My memory bank went blank, totally and completely insufficient. My hands got sweaty, my mouth went dry, and my husband watched me stumble.

He patted my shoulder, rubbed his tummy, extended his hand, and said, "Bill, my name's Bill." Then he winked at me. I made an appointment with the doctor. She asked me to spell the word "world" backwards, and she put me through a slew of memory tests. She ruled out Alzheimer's and welcomed me to the world of brief brain blips and memory slips called senior citizenship. As long as I can remember my own name, I think I'll be all okay.

Section III
Covert Body Changes

"A healthy body means a healthy mind.
You get your heart rate up, and you get the blood
flowing through your body to your brain. Look at
Albert Einstein. He rode a bicycle. He was also an early
student of Jazzercise. You never saw Einstein lift his
shirt, but he had a six-pack under there."

—STEVE CARELL

The Wax Museum

Eileen Mitchell

Whatever happened to Baby Jane is starting to happen to me. I'm not talking about serving up parakeets on a platter (not yet), like Bette Davis did to Joan Crawford in that twisted cinematic tale of sisterly rivalry gone to the birds. I'm talking about a jolt far more frightening than any horror flick frenzy. I'm referring to the monumental moment in the mirror when girlish becomes ghoulish (or boyish becomes *oyish*). Suddenly the look that worked for so long is now so unworkable. The porcelain complexion has faded from translucent to Transylvanian—the wax museum is calling your name. For men, aging is a simple matter of accepting a bad toupee and stocking up on luau shirts. For women it's a little more complex, like having a youthful replica of yourself, courtesy of Madame Tussauds, fitted with a wick and lit with a blowtorch, and you get to watch while it melts.

Forget about crinkles and crow's feet—your complexion will soon resemble a crepe de chine blouse, which is the most fashionable thing one can say about your appearance. When your skin starts to sag more than your sweat pants, you begin to wonder: can housecoats and babushkas be far off?

Your creamy white throat is still tempting, but not in the way it used to be. The resemblance to turkey skin makes you hungry (what doesn't?), but now you get to accessorize your wardrobe with a wattle. For the rich and famous, aging poses no problems because looking like a mutant freak is apparently considered chic in Hollywood. For regular humans, however, some semblance of humanoid features is required to successfully co-mingle in society. And besides, the average budget doesn't allow for anything other than Oil of Olay. Heck, forget about the budget, you pass out at the dentist—are you really going to let someone inject toxins into your body (other than whipped cream and spray cheese)? Botox brow and collagen lips may work on the red carpet, but in real life, children are so easily frightened. Cultivating a colorful personality profile is a far more realistic solution for the not-so-rich and far-from-famous. For men, becoming a spunky geezer is always a popular option. Single gals can consider the cat-lady lifestyle. Classic choices for moms include: Muumuu Mom—billowy dresses, crinkled hair, and bosomy hugs; Manic Mom—glued-on grin, piercing pitch, and busy-bee bravado; or Matronly Mom—plump, placid, and proper. Or you could go full-out eccentric (Norma Desmond style), and become Madcap Mom sporting age-inappropriate clothes, embarrassing dance moves, and hop-on-a-motorcycle-just-before-you-break-your-hip joie de vivre. Whoever you are and whatever you choose, remember your new mantra: *no one will notice your crinkles and frownies, if you keep them distracted with cookies and brownies.*

Ode to a Speculum

Maxine Jeffris

One of the benefits of being a woman of a "certain age" is that I rarely get my nether regions examined anymore. Perhaps I am unusual in this, but I do not miss lying on a paper runner like a slab of bacon waiting to be wrapped. Nor do I miss the old stainless steel speculum kept in a bucket of ice water.

After one of those yearly double-exposures I wrote a poem, of which I am ever so proud.

In fact, I think I can say with complete modesty that I have suffered for my art. Now, dear reader, it is your turn.

Ode to a Speculum

Maxine Jeffris

With my feet up in the stirrups,
Full moon shining to the west,
I lie shivering on the table,
Paper gown clutched to my breast.
And while the doctor sits and tinkers
With his head between my knees,
I imagine how surprised he'd look
If I gave his head a squeeze.

Brenda Elsagher

Then he picks up this contraption,
All covered o'er with frost,
And approaches the sacred portal . . .
that far too few have crossed.
Then he pulls me gently forward
With a firm grip on my hips,
And says, "There, are you comfy?"
I think, "Hey Doc, read my lips!"

My Winter of Discontent

PAMELA GOLDSTEIN

After retiring in 1994, one thing had become abundantly clear to me: I hate winter. I hate being cold. I hate hearing my aching, arthritic joints creak when I wake up on cold winter mornings. I also hate having to wear an undershirt under the regular shirt under the vest under the sweater under the winter jacket, with a scarf around my throat, a scarf around my face, a hat on my head with earmuffs over the hat.

And that's just to take out the garbage.

However, none of this has ever deterred me from making the same two New Year's resolutions with my friend Carol every year: lose weight, exercise more. We're both diabetics, and naturally our doctors harp on us to do these two things. So . . . Zumba, but Carol fell and broke her arm. We decided maybe this wasn't our thing. Weights, but I have arthritis in my back and shoulders, so it is too painful. Swimming; we both love swimming, but the only times pools in our area are available for swimming lengths is seven or eight in the morning, when neither of us is even awake, or after ten in the evening. Hello, we turned the TV on at eight and fell asleep within ten minutes of our favorite show starting.

We decided not to be discouraged from our lofty goals. We vowed last New Year's Eve that this was the year we would succeed, by golly, or else our names would be *mush*. We agreed we would walk every morning for an hour, no matter what. Yup! Easy peasy.

New Year's Day, and we're pumped for our first one-hour walk for a new decade, a new year, and a new regimen.

"I'll finish my Special K and be right over," says Carol.

"I'll be ready."

I start layering. I'm up to the sweater over the shirt when I have to pee. Urgency is yet another challenge and joy of aging, and it gives me a new thrill—making it to the bathroom before disaster strikes and a puddle appears on the floor in front of the toilet. Whew, this time was close. Now, back to the pants.

Ten minutes later, I'm at the door having the Hot Flash from Hell.

Carol arrives in a frantic state. "I have to pee!" she cries as she strips out of her clothes and runs for the bathroom.

"Take your time," I say. Meanwhile, there's a pool of sweat around me; I'm melting. Nobody ever mentioned that those hot flashes from menopause continue for the rest of your life.

Finally, we're outside and walking. It's snowing.

"It sure is brisk out here," I say after a few minutes. My nostrils have frozen shut and my teeth are chattering. I have to pee, but I'm determined to overcome the urge.

"What? I can't hear you through my hat and earmuffs," shouts Carol. "I'm freezing my butt off!" She grabs my arm. "We have to go back. I have to pee again!"

After we pare down to one shirt and pair of pants, I light a fire in the fireplace and make us hot cocoa with whipping cream.

Carol sighs. "We walked a lousy seven minutes. A disaster! Why did we think we could exercise in winter?" We each raise a can of whipping cream in salute to our failure and fill our mouths. "Next year, let's resolve to write a novel. We might keep that resolution."

"If we don't run out of hot cocoa and whipping cream," I reply, "at least we won't be cold, and we'll be close to the washroom."

"But we'll gain a ton of weight," muttered Carol.

I sigh and look at the now-empty can of whipping cream. MUSH, my name is MUSH.

The Helicopter

BRENDA ELSAGHER

Losing weight is a challenge for most people, and having been overweight most of my adult life, it took until I was fifty-three when the stars must have aligned for me to seriously work on it. Things are different when you lose weight in your fifties because the elasticity in your skin you took for granted in your younger years is long gone.

When I had a nice plump face, I never had wrinkles except laugh lines around my eyes. These days, with a leaner face, come tons of wrinkles. So my body looks younger, I'm just not so sure about my face. You know those Shar Pei dogs and how you can push their skin forward to get an old-man dog look? There are some similarities between us.

I can walk a lot faster these days; I just have to wait a minute for my skin to catch up. And other things started happening to my body. I was lying in bed next to my husband and I felt a lump on my chest. Of course I paid attention because my sister and mother are both breast cancer survivors, so I asked my husband to feel the lump.

He explored it, and with a serious look, he said, "Brenda, I think I know what it is."

"What do you think?"

"I believe they call this your sternum."

"This is a sternum? I've never felt it before. Are you sure?"

"I'm positive; these are things that show up when you are a hundred fifty pounds smaller, Brenda."

"Well, it probably helps that my boobs are not where they used to be and don't really stay in one place anymore."

"Your boobs are fine; you are fine. I love you." Gotta love that man.

A few days later, after a shower, I was reaching for a towel while looking in the mirror at the same time. I saw something move, so I reached again. Oh my gosh, this must be a pectoral muscle. I didn't know I had one. Yes, the little things make me excited.

Being more like a normal size these days, I have much more energy and flexibility. Not too long ago I decided to tackle a thorough cleaning of the shower. Using bleach, and not wanting to ruin my clothes with accidental splashes, I decided to go naked as I cleaned.

Just as I was scrubbing away, I heard a helicopter overhead, sounding dangerously close. *Whop, whop, whop* went the blades of the helicopter. I stopped and listened to how close it was, feeling a little self-conscious being naked in my bathroom as it was right over my house.

When it moved on, I went back doing a great job of scrubbing. Then I heard it—the *whop, whop, whop* was appearing to get closer. I stopped scrubbing immediately and wondered, Should I grab a towel and go look out the window? Just when I started my internal conversation, the helicopter went away again.

Back to scrubbing I went, and soon realized in an awkward instant the *whop, whop, whop* I had been hearing was in fact the skin hanging from my upper arm, which almost seemed disconnected. It was flapping through the air with my strong movements, making the same exact sound of *whop, whop, whop* like a helicopter.

I quit cleaning the shower after this incident.

Mirror Image

CHERYL JOBE

It amazes me—everyone around me is aging and oh, how it shows. I ran into an old friend while buying groceries not long ago and was stunned by the gray hair and all those wrinkles.

"It's so good to see you," I said, "but you look so tired, have you been ill?"

She drew back as if I were holding a snake. "Of course not! I see my doctor regularly, do yoga four times a week, and I'm coaching my grandson in tennis every weekend. He's very good, and his future looks bright. And you, what do you do with yourself these days?"

I was at a loss for an answer; do I make up a life of adventure? Or tell the truth? Could I really tell her I work the crossword puzzle in the newspaper each day, followed by household chores before falling asleep at 9:00 p.m. each evening in front of the T.V.?

So I took the wimpy road, "Oh, I stay busy with this and that, sorry, gotta run."

I thought about it all the way home. My friend had looked old; she has to be at least three years younger than I am. I carried in my purchases and put them away, still thinking of our chance meeting. I may not be as physically active, but I look years younger.

An hour later my husband came in from his workshop, and as we sat down to lunch I told him of my morning's experience. He said, "You know, that's funny. I ran into a former co-worker at the hardware store earlier, and I was shocked. His jowls were sagging, stomach too, and he's almost completely bald now." We shook our heads at what was going on with those around us. After lunch he went for a nap, and I settled in for the afternoon talk shows, only slightly annoyed when our oldest daughter stopped in for a visit.

I had never noticed the varicose veins sprouting from under the hem of her capris, or the loose skin along her upper arms.

Come to think of it, the roots of her auburn hair were more white than dark. I must have been staring as she said, "Mom, are you okay? You look like you've never seen me before."

"No, no I'm fine; I just realized you're looking old these days."

She laughed, and reminded me that if she was showing her age, I was twenty-four years older.

"Nonsense," I said. "I look like I always have; I can't see that I look any different than I did ten or twenty years ago."

Ever the know-it-all, my daughter remarked, "Either you need new glasses, or your mirrors need cleaning."

Mirrors? I'd forgotten about those. We had only two in the house, and I didn't think to look in them. They weren't needed to brush my dentures, or to twist my hair up into its usual knot every morning. I could dress myself without them because I knew my clothes fit. To tell the truth, I couldn't remember the last time I'd looked in a mirror. Yes, I looked at them when I cleaned them, but not at the person doing the cleaning.

Taking my arm, this old-woman daughter of mine led me into the bathroom and stood me before the vanity mirror. I looked, squinted, turned my head this way and that, took my glasses off and looked, then put them back on and looked again. Finally it soaked in: while I wasn't looking, a wrinkled and gray person had come in and taken over my body. Nothing was where it had been; it had all slid down my bones. Then my mind's eye pictured my husband: the beard he kept neatly trimmed was now white, and tufts of hair had grown from his nostrils and ears. His chest was now in the area of his stomach, and bags had grown under his eyes.

Okay, it had crept up on me—I am that old lady in the mirror. Just wait until he gets up from his nap, *have I got a surprise for him.*

The Price Tag

BRENDA ELSAGHER

Becoming a comedian at age forty, I achieved one of my bucket-list items. Many unusual things came out of the goal that led me to becoming a professional speaker. I found I could talk about serious subjects in a respectful yet hilarious manner. I was asked by the American Cancer Society to speak at a fundraising dinner. I knew our former Minnesota Governor Arne Carlson would also be speaking, and I wanted to look my best for such a prestigious event.

I had a black dress I was considering, and heard about a boutique that carried pretty little scarves and vests, and thought I might get something to dress it up with a little color. The sales women were extremely helpful and accommodating, and brought me several things to consider. They were friendly, almost fawning over me, and I told them about giving a talk where the governor was going to be, which seemed to inspire them more. We all decided a flowy hand-painted silk vest would be the perfect complement to the dress.

I stole a quick glance at the price of $200, which is a lot to spend. I didn't even spend that much on my wedding dress. Then I talked myself into it, rationalizing . . . I'm sure I'll use this on many occasions.

They had told me about the artist who painted it, calling it wearable art. I thought it was precious, and told myself I was worth it. Justifications in place, I walked to the cashier and handed her my charge card.

She said matter-of-factly, "That will be $2,000, and no tax because it's clothing."

I stammered, "Whaaaattttt? It's $2,000? I was debating over $200, apparently I didn't read the price tag correctly. I'm sorry, I can't afford that."

I left the store in a hurry, and when I had my eyes examined the next day, I learned I needed reading glasses.

May the Flash Be with You

Laurie Fabrizio

Q: What's more disturbing than road rage, soggier than a wet newspaper, and nastier than the moldy mystery food in the refrigerator?

Q: What warms your body faster than a quick shot of tequila?

The answer: a hot flash, your perfect personal heating system. Your body surface temperature is a steady one thousand degrees. You could cook popcorn in your cleavage. No need to stop at the movie concession stand. Your continuous glow has people thinking: "She just had a facial," or "She had plastic surgery." The only work I had done was housework.

I'm over fifty, and suffer from an incessant dewy complexion and the "just out of the washer" look. I have patented the glow with a daily facial. My face is patted with a towel, and dried with my personal mini fan. I painstakingly apply makeup, pausing to dab at the beading sweat. After lacquering on the final coat, the mini fan dries my efforts. On a good day, I look great for ten minutes, before it melts off like a slushy.

There isn't makeup suitable for menopausal women. Foundation turns you into Yoda on a good day. Stick to powder eye shadow unless you want to be mistaken for Lady Gaga. Animal control mistakes you for a raccoon when your mascara and eyeliner smudge. The hot flash nabs you anytime, especially during a shopping excursion. I recently found the perfect blazer. Would it be inappropriate to go topless underneath?

Flagging down a salesgirl, I needed a viable solution. "This turtleneck would make the outfit pop," she said perkily. Seriously? Maybe I'll also purchase a sauna on the way out.

"Miss, do you have something less heat retaining?"

"How about this cable knit V-neck sweater?"

By now the beads of sweat were doing the Electric Slide on my forehead. I spied a sleeveless camisole, and grabbed it before another menopausal woman snatched it. Shopping was just too stressful.

This winter I decided the only way to preserve all of my painstaking makeup efforts was to keep the house cooler. Unfortunately the hot flashes prevailed. Hubby felt like he was living with "wifezilla." The neighbors reported me for streaking outside, wearing only a tank top and underwear. Heaven help me if I have a glass of wine. One sip, and I resemble a drenched dog.

One night, I crawled into bed, the winter gales howling outside. The bedroom window was ajar, heat turned down to sixty degrees, and I was donning a short-sleeved T-shirt. Hubby was huddled under the covers, in a down jacket, spooning a king-size down pillow.

"Cripes, it's five degrees outside; can you close the damn window?" He nudged the pillow aside, and threw another log on the fire. "You could hang meat in here," he said through frosted breath. Hmm . . . hadn't thought of that. Come to think of it, I was a little short on freezer space.

"I'm as warm as hot-buttered rum," I said, purring while perched on top of the mountains of blankets he had scrounged.

Hubby was considering a space heater until I convinced him it would set the mattress on fire. Next thing I knew I caught him rubbing two sticks together over the pages he tore out of my latest book club material.

Seeing my hubby was on the verge of delirium and hypothermia, I relented and closed the window. Our bedroom fan runs twenty-four/seven, and I now sleep in tank top and shorts. Hubby has learned to wrap himself in a parka as he exits the shower, knowing I will have the bathroom window ajar. He ducks past my personal fan before icicles begin to form on his nose and his ear hair while his dreams of installing a steam shower have been washed down the drain.

After ingesting countless homeopathic remedies, trying various medications, and succumbing to a battery of tests, my doctor phoned to assure me I was not losing my mind. Apparently my body chose to go straight into menopause. No lines, no waiting. The doctor decided to prescribe a combo hormone patch. I needed something to put my hormones on cruise control.

"Does that mean I'll grow facial hair other than the rogue chin hair I pluck every week?" The doctor assured me the patch would stabilize my hormones to where they should be when one is going through menopause.

The good news: I no longer keep the window open in the middle of winter. You may actually now see me in public sporting a long-sleeve top. From force of habit, I never zip up my jacket. The family is relieved I no longer attack with "that look" when someone eats the last chocolate chip cookie.

The bad news: I have crop circles all over my stomach from the sticky patch residue. When the History Channel show *America Unearthed* contacted me for an interview, I assured them this was not a UFO sighting.

Your Glasses Are on Top of Your Head

There is hope. As I peruse the spring catalogs, I visualize myself in something other than sleeveless tops. I'm sick of seeing my flabby upper arms anyway. With summer around the corner, my hubby will inevitably catch a break. I'll keep the air conditioner at a balmy sixty-eight degrees. The meat normally hanging in our bedroom will be relegated to the freezer. Neighbors may be relieved they no longer have to hear my husband's expletives when the electric bill arrives. My streaking escapades will be curtailed, so as not to frighten small children.

"Hot flash" sounds so sexy and seductive; it could be the name for an exotic dancer. Perspiring doesn't make me feel sexy. To those of you in the cosmetic industry, give us fifty-plus menopausal women a break. How about introducing waterproof makeup? Just because we may enjoy *Singing in the Rain* doesn't mean we want to look like drowned rats. Or how about a menopausal clothing line for women "of a certain age," with fabrics designed to wick away the moisture and have a cooling gel center?

Perhaps it is a state of mind. Ladies, you are not alone in your sultry moments. May the "Flash" be with you all.

Dare to Enter

T'Mara Goodsell

The cute auburn-haired young woman at the Department of Motor Vehicles spoke in a rapid-fire script:

"I need your old driver's license, two pieces of identification, and proof of residency."

I was ready for her and proud of it. I'd been on a marathon chore run since the morning, and had prepared lists, maps, coupons, addresses, and DMV-requested ID in advance in order to make it all possible. I had all the license renewal papers separated in a little file folder, labeled with a sticky note. Matching her beat, I slid the folder at her.

"Your license, ma'am?" she asked, making an audible eye roll.

"Oh. Of course."

Boom. Stamp. I was a well-oiled machine, moving with smooth and silent precision. I'd get my license renewed in record time, and my hair didn't look too bad for my new photo. She told me to read the line in the machine.

I still have flashbacks to the last time. I'd waited until the last possible moment, rushed out there after work on my birthday, confident I could get it done quickly. I was overwhelmed in those days, in the middle of my forties, and the middle of a divorce at the same time. The last time, when I looked in the machine to read the letters, it was broken. When I told the clerk, she just froze and gawked at me, like someone had thrown a wrench into her mechanical speech.

"Ma'am, it isn't broken. Were you pressing down with your forehead? Try again."

I did. The realization and the horror hit at the same time as the hot flash crept up from my knees through my torso and up into my face. I could feel myself sweating on the viewfinder thing that must be the granddaddy of the little View-Masters I played with as a child, inserting little pineapple-slice slides to reveal the 3-D picture. My favorite was Wile E. Coyote.

But there was no 3-D picture there. No Wile E. No E, even. Just a big blur where the letters should have been. Again and again, I tried to will those letters to appear, dreading the humiliation of having to look up at the clerk. She was now the speech-delivering machine, and I was the old, clunky broken part sunk into the works, stopping everything up. As if from a distance, I heard her telling me my license was *denied,* and I needed to get glasses and then come back. She said it with an audible "duh" in her voice.

She handed me a temporary license, and I stumbled out in a daze. Glasses? I'd never worn glasses in my life. Now I was old, alone, and blind, too. And on my birthday. I cried all the way home, compounding my blindness even further.

Now I'm a regular pro, whipping on my glasses automatically just before turning the key in the ignition. At the return eye exam at the DMV, I was proud to rattle those letters right off. Whew. *I was hot.* Well, maybe not hot, but on the ball. Then came the signs on the machine.

I always forget about the road signs. I worry about everything else, so the signs catch me off guard. I was moving, I was doing well, I was getting through the line in record time, so I figured I could handle the signs I've been reading most of my life: No Left Turn, Yield, Merge. And then there it was, staring me in the face. What on earth was it called? I couldn't remember. I knew what it meant—I just couldn't for the life of me remember the official name. Just as flashbacks of the vision test debacle crept in, the pressure was too much and I spilled out, "Oh, you know—it means, 'Don't go there.'"

Oh crap, oh crap. *Don't go there?!* I had just gone there all right . . . to Senileville. She would probably revoke my license for good this time. But she did know what I meant, thank heavens. Maybe she was used to people my age renaming signs. Or maybe she threw it in as a gift for having all of my papers in a neat little paisley-print folder with matching sticky note.

Regardless, she nodded and efficiently dispatched me down the counter. "Next?"

My new picture on my license looks like a mug shot where the criminal can't believe she got caught. For the next few years, I will carry around a picture where I look like I'm perpetually saying, "Huh?"

I will always know what I was thinking: What the hell do you call that stupid sign? It's right on the tip of my tongue.

Once I was safely in my car, I broke down again, this time in laughter. As I exited the parking lot, I suddenly screamed, *"Do not enter!"*

Good thing no one was around to hear me, or I might have caused an accident. Old age is driving me to distraction. Might as well don my glasses and enjoy the ride.

Got Game?

Barb Best

Advancing age humbles you. Humility requires you to accept these things: you have faults, you are not always the best, and you must remain open to improvement. So, I ask you, what better way to develop your humbler self than playing a competitive sport after age fifty?

Tennis, anyone? What used to qualify as a leisurely hobby for you now becomes a battle of wits, fits, snits, and occasional quits. Since you are no longer a spring chicken (and who is these days?), you must consider the following when lacing up to play: health insurance is a racket, but you can't play without a racquet. Don't leave home without either.

Hard, bouncy balls are happy balls. Flexibility is more important than mere raw power. Reach, stretch, bend, and pull the muscle. Snap. Ouch! Wince and repeat. "Start with *love,* and serve all" is a great philosophy—on and off the court. "*Love, love*" is a nifty sentiment in scoring, plus it's fun to say. "*Love, love, love, love.*" Spin is everything. Lay it on.

Expect muscle pain before, during, and after playing; especially if you have arthritis, joint reconstructions, osteoporosis, bursitis, or low magnesium. Ibuprofen is your best friend. No pain, no game. The importance of play to mental health is understated, as is the agony of defeat. Also, the agony of the feet. You will learn plantar fasciitis is not a veggie pasta dish.

The worst thing you can do (other than have a massive coronary while lunging for a low one at the net) is fall, trip, roll, collide, or otherwise cause yourself to break something, *anything*—especially a bone. After all, bones don't grow on trees. If you suffer a fracture, you will not be able to play for weeks, months, or maybe years. This will cause you a heap of emotional pain on top of your chronic body aches, and most likely motivate you to excessively drink vodka and carbonated beverages.

Did you know? With advanced age, there are special rules for tennis: If you're over fifty years old, there's no shame if you only run for the ball 75 percent of the time—or when you're really in the mood. If you're over sixty, don't be embarrassed. You can save the remaining cartilage in your shoulder by serving underhand instead of overhand. If you're over seventy, guess what? You're no longer expected to remember the score. Bonus: this increases your opportunities for inadvertently cheating. And if you're over eighty, no sweat. You get two bounces to return every ball. Also, you don't have to shower after playing.

Frequent breaks for the restroom and change of attire will be allowed. Can you say, "Bladder unpredictability?" A sun-visor is required. Chances are you can't see so well anyway, let alone if the sun is smack dab in your eyes. Chalk this one up to "function over fashion." Cap sleeves are not allowed as arm jangles and bat wings cause a distraction to the other players, and freak out nearby children. Great shots in tennis include, but are not limited to: vitamin B12, cortisone, steroids, pain killers, wrinkle fillers, passing shot, drop shot, lob, slice, smash, vodka . . . in that order.

Bragging rights are encouraged.

"Damn I'm good. I beat a fifty-nine-year-old last week."

"We finished a whole set. Not bad for a bunch of old ladies."

"Look. My grip is tight as a camel's ass."

Remember: "As long as you have a hobby or a sport, you have a purpose." You may knit this slogan on a therapy pillow, and take it to your rheumatologist appointments. Playing tennis in your later years? It's a triumph of the lagging spirit and the sagging spine. All together now: just say "No!" to tennis balls on orthopedic walkers.

A Midlife Crisis Should Be More Fun

DOROTHY ROSBY

I was thirty-six when I had my only child, and I soon discovered the advantages of being an older mom: I was suddenly a member of an elite group. Julia Roberts, Madonna, and Susan Sarandon all had babies long after the old biological clock needed new batteries. At crowded school programs, younger mothers let me take the last remaining chair. And by the time I'm actually a grandmother, I'll be accustomed to being called one.

But there are disadvantages, too, the main one being that having an adolescent boy and a perimenopausal mother under the same roof is like storing the matches with the dynamite. On the bright side, my son and I are getting moustaches at the same time. We're both suffering through our own versions of Hormone Hell, but today, we'll focus on mine. He might be embarrassed if I write about his.

The way I see it, estrogen is a sometimes benevolent, sometimes cruel dictator ruling a woman's life from puberty until menopause. When we reach a certain age, estrogen starts to relinquish its power, leaving behind a dangerous leadership vacuum, and causing crises in our midlife crises that are not nearly as much fun as we had hoped they would be.

Take me, for example. Instead of getting a tattoo, I got a middle-aged middle. On the bright side, I *do* have more room for tattoos.

Instead of a career change, I had a personality change. I've become increasingly impatient and irritable to strangers, behavior I once reserved for the people I love.

Instead of a new sports car, I got a new thermostat, and I don't mean for the house. My whole life, I've been a cold person. I don't mean cold as in cold-hearted cold, no matter what the previously mentioned strangers say. I mean cold as in long-johns-from-October-to-June cold. And I still am, except when I'm not, like at random, inconvenient times throughout the day and night. I've come to believe global warming was brought on by the hot flashes of the Baby Boom generation.

My good friend Google tells me this could go on for years. I'm afraid when I finally get through it, my family will have moved out. I won't have any friends left. All I'll have to show for my ordeal is greater body mass and more facial hair. Just like my son.

Look for the Positive

MICHELE WOOD

There comes a time in life when a woman might worry, or rejoice, because she sounds or acts just like her mother. Never did I imagine I'd act *like my mother-in-law*. My in-laws were snowbirds in Arizona, and going out meant having a midday meal. This really translated to driving in the daylight, less traffic, and visiting establishments catering to their fine sensibilities, a.k.a. senior discounts.

On a drive, my mother-in-law noticed a sign and said, "Look, that's interesting!"

"What?" Pop replied.

"Fried seal lips."

Pop looked and burst out laughing. "Dear, it says fried scallops. Who would serve fried seal lips?"

In her defense, some electric cables were obscuring the sign. She was mortified because fried seal lips did seem ridiculous, and she made him promise not to tell anyone. Instead it became standard ribbing material about her little failing visual acuity, which she loathed.

Recently I have also read signs incorrectly. While visiting my husband in the hospital, I saw a sign reading Micro Morbidity Center. I kept thinking and wondering, what was it? A tiny stroke center? A center for negative outcomes? Flummoxed, I blamed my lack of understanding on being away from higher education too long.

The next day when I returned and got a little closer, I read it accurately: Micro Mobility Center. It had nothing to do with morbidity at all; I had to laugh at myself and my active imagination.

I am thankful after thirty-six years of marriage that neither of us can see once the glasses come off. This "gift" allows us to still share a bath and bedroom. I thought the term fading beauty was poetic until the actual fading, or the disappearance of pigment happened where I live. Gray hair hasn't bothered me, in fact it suits me; it's as blond as I will ever be. Random whiskers or ropey long neck hairs are hard to see. The touch method is a better way to find them. While I seldom text and drive, I do tweeze and drive. If you read about an accident where the driver was impaled with tweezers, it might be me.

I wish someone would explain to me why the outer third of my eyebrows disappeared, and simply stopped growing. Meanwhile, the remaining brows sprout out like Jack in the Bean Stalk, wiry, silver lengths I may as well bead rather than color with pencil or powder. They require trimming often, like fast-growing bushes.

My skin seems to get paler everywhere, and will no longer tan. Instead, brown spots of varying sizes on my face, arms, and hands appear. Two splotches, little brown islands, now occupy the real estate where my brows once lived, the bane of my existence. Perhaps I can be a connect-the-dot game with the grandkids.

Strength and stature have always been important. Not position or status. I'm talking posture, height; we're big people. My husband is 6 foot, 8 inches, and I am 5 foot, 8 inches. Thus we have a king-sized bed. As years have gone by, our bed, once a playground, is now more like a parking lot with well-worn, identified spaces where we each roll into nightly. My husband says our bed is a metaphor for docking boats, each with our own slip in which to slide and moor with covers rather than ropes— at least for now. Whoever gets up last makes the bed each day. We straighten covers, restack pillows, and smooth the spread over the top, while two canoe-shaped depressions remain.

We laugh a lot, and work at looking for the positive, while little irritations are quickly forgotten. We let slip into momentary obscurity nearly everything except the oldest of tales, the ones we've told each other too often. One of the more exciting findings of memory loss is we can meet new people every day, and this really makes for great adventures.

It never ceases to surprise us when a stranger feels the need to remind us of our age. Recently, I needed to purchase a couple of bags of salt for the water softener. The cashier commented as she signaled the bagger, "He can load and take those to your car."

"No, I can do it," I said.

More insistent, she said, "It's no problem, he can help you."

"I'm strong! I've got it." I struck a body builder's pose. The guy in the line behind me clapped.

At the deli counter my husband inquired, "What's the best potato salad?"

The clerk replied, "The old people like this one."

He paused and asked, "Which one do you like?"

She said, "I don't like potato salad."

He ordered slaw.

Living in the Midwest, winters can last a long time, made even longer when the sun doesn't shine. Gray days are a lot worse than gray hair, always have been. Silliness and surprise are necessary tools for coping. Sharing real-life antics with friends, and laughing, are essential to my well-being. Trying to coax a lighter mood one afternoon, I rummaged to find the unused Breathe Right strips, which had not stopped the snoring. My husband was lucky enough to find good-fitting earplugs to drown out my imitation of a freight train.

Longing for light and lost youth, I pulled up the fluffy overhang of tissue above my eye. I secured the adhesive end of the Breathe Right tab, and then pulled upward at a thirty-degree slant before taping the butterfly-esque end to my hair line. Miracle of miracles, my plan worked, I could see more, and there was light. Quickly correcting the other side, I showed my husband my low-cost facelift. He became Ricky Ricardo of the *Lucy* show, shaking his head, muttering, "Aye, aye, aye!"

Laughter gets us through it all.

The Surprises of Menopause

VIKKI CLAFLIN

Google "benefits of menopause" and you'll get 8,570,000 possible links with as many articles written on how menopause makes us stronger, sexier, more confident, and more at peace with our bodies and our sexuality. Not to mention the exhilarating freedom from periods, bloating, cramping, PMS, and the constant worry about pregnancy—however slim the chance.

What they don't tell you in those same posts is all that Zen is achieved after menopause is over. It's the prize at the end of a rather bumpy ride, during which you'll start questioning whether you'll ever be sexy again—or if you even care.

Like most women, I like feeling attractive, sexy, and desirable. I've spent more money than I probably should've toward this goal over the years, and although yoga pants and no makeup are my norm, I do clean up fairly well, which admittedly takes longer with each passing year. I have a tiny but persistent inner hot chick who still likes stilettos, little black dresses, and the appreciative looks from my husband at my efforts. Menopause crashed my hotness with a thud heard in three states.

Suddenly I was more "ma'am" than a woman who men would lust after. Men stopped whistling at me from the street, and started helping me through the crosswalk. People no longer commented, "You look so much like your mother," and started assuming we were sisters. One unfortunate store owner in town asked me if I was my son's grandmother. (As soon as I figure out how to hide the body, he's going to die.)

In retrospect, I'm amazed my husband made it through my menopausal years. He married a reasonably confident, arguably normal woman, and woke up one day to an overheated, moody, questionably sane female sobbing uncontrollably over the sudden appearance of cankles. My young sexiness was gone. Menopause killed it with hot flashes. We were out at our favorite romantic restaurant, and the coy flirting of our early years—"Gee, Big Guy, is it hot in here or is it just you?"—became, "Is it hot in here or what? I'm hot. Is anybody else hot?"

Repeated requests to the uncooperative waiter to turn the thermostat down finally ended with a screeching, "Can't you turn the freaking heat down? It's *too friggin' hot in here.*" My husband dragged my sweaty body out of the restaurant, and we haven't been back since.

And then there were the metabolism changes. Actually, mine didn't change. It stopped. Weight maintenance was now limited to one Fruit Loop and a Diet Coke per day. Weight loss required colonic cleansing and fasting. And if you like wine, no carbs for you. Ever. Carbs plus wine make you blow up like a puffer fish, so you have to choose. I haven't had a carb since 2009.

Fatigue was next. I was tired all the time. Bedtime went from 10:30 p.m. to 8:30 p.m., effectively eliminating boogie nights on the dance floor, since it's virtually impossible to find a band starting at 5:30.

Night sweats followed. Yeah, nothing turns a man on more than being whacked on the arm at 2 a.m. to "get up" because we have to change the cold, wet sheets. Again. After the first six months, we both got used to just tossing beach towels over the sheets and crawling back into bed. Take that, sex life.

The next delightful surprise was day sweats. I quit going to the gym after realizing my clothes would be soaked, with visible sweat pouring down between my boobs and my butt crack, and I'd been on the treadmill for only three minutes. It took me longer to wipe down the machine than it did to work out.

Then the delightful incontinence came along. I'd laugh. A little squirt. I'd sneeze. Another little squirt. The actual need to pee? Now I'd be clenching my muscles while I waddle-ran to the nearest bathroom, praying there wasn't a line, and fully prepared to bust into the men's room if necessary. By the end of the evening, I smelled like Eau de Pee, sitting in wet undies, and wondering what the hell had happened to my life. Hubby, not surprisingly, was still not turned on.

Next in line were the mood swings. Some days, my husband would come home to find me sobbing over yet another Hallmark commercial about the son returning home at Christmas to his adoring little sister and happy, teary-eyed parents. Other days, any and all comments directed at me, from anyone in the room, on any subject, were met with, "What the hell is wrong with you?" accompanied, when the stupidity level warranted it, by a smack upside the head. Hubby claimed later every day was a crap shoot.

Physical changes weren't pretty. Under-arm twaddle, boobs headed toward my knees, and hips widening irrevocably eliminated anything sleeveless or low-cut from my closet, and would forevermore require military-grade underwear. Menopause underwear is designed to git 'er done, by pushing, lifting, and shoving defiant and migrating body parts back into their original shape and place. We no longer care about lace edging or cute bows. We need underwire that could double for an internet connection and a strong elastic company on speed-dial.

Body heat. I was basically just hot. All. The. Time. We had the front door open year-round, and unless it was raining, I had the top down on my car—in December. I turned the house heat completely off every night, and opened the windows. My husband repeatedly complained he couldn't perform in a refrigerator. I reminded him once it's a bad chef who blames his utensils, but apparently he didn't get my humor. Nobody got any that night.

Hunger came along, and I was always hungry. And somehow, I have no recollection of craving carrots. I do remember threatening my hubby one night for eating the last of my Milk Duds. To this day, he's never eaten another Dud.

Evening conversations tended more toward chronic menopausal-induced irritable bowel syndrome than pleasantly discussing our mutual plans for our next vacation through the wine country. My husband, who's not once in fifteen years seen me pee because I want to maintain a modicum of mystery in our marriage, looked a bit stunned one night when I bent over and hiked up the back of my dress, asking, "When I bend over like this, can you see cellulite on the backs of my legs?" He laughed so hard he fell off his chair, but was smart enough to leave the question untouched.

Now, at the end of the tunnel, I'm approaching inner peace. But it was a humbling and often mortifying ride. And occasionally, when I'm doing my morning prayers and meditation, my thoughts will free-fall back to those years and I'll ask God, "Really?"

I'm still waiting for a response.

Section IV
Family Wisdom

"The day the child realizes that all adults are imperfect he becomes an adolescent; the day he forgives them, he becomes an adult; the day he forgives himself he becomes wise."

—ALDEN NOWLAN, *BETWEEN TEARS AND LAUGHTER*

The Not-So-Subtle Shifts of Getting Older

RICK ELSEN

My friend Larry and I go way back. We like to remember when we were in our thirties when the closest thing to a medical discussion might be about the cute nurse we met at a singles dance. Now every time we get together it seems like a fifteen-minute recital of our appointments, medications, blood pressure, cholesterol levels, and our latest colonoscopy report.

Maybe it's just me, but as the hair on my head gets thinner, it seems to find new homes. I have to continuously shave hairs on my nose and around the outside edges of my ears, trim inside my ears and nostrils, and find tufts growing from my shoulders. I don't even want to talk about what happens on my rear.

I used to be able to take a tough tackle while playing football, or slide hard and fast into base during a game, which caused me to walk with a limp all day. Now the act of getting out of bed can be enough.

When I was thirty, I used to wish for a little gray hair to make me look more mature, credible, and distinguished; now at age sixty, I can hardly be distinguished from all the other white-haired men in the room.

I knew I was making an impression with my age sounds when my two-year-old granddaughter thought she also had to go "Augghh" every time she got out of the chair.

I used to be able to stop shaving and cutting my hair in the fall, and put on a plaid shirt and be a macho Grizzly Adams sort of guy. Now when I do it, they give me a red suit, and I play Santa Claus.

We do a lot of traveling, and one evening in Italy, our group went to a small restaurant that had live music and dancing. A beautiful young Italian woman asked me to dance, and after a couple of dances, she whispered in my ear during a slow song. When I returned to the table, one of the people wanted to know what she said.

I told them, "My Italian isn't very good, but I don't think she was inviting me for a romantic evening. I think she said, 'You remind me of my Grandpa.'"

Peepaw New

Cindy Barefield

My father-in-law (Peepaw) was born in 1918. Having survived the Depression years, he had a keen sense of recycling and thriftiness. Although he might not seem successful, he rarely called a repairman to the house. Same mantra in the kitchen. Julia Child he was not, but he always ate what he cooked—*burned or not*. Our family developed a saying about anything he might want to give you. He would describe it as brand new or almost new, and when you got it, it might be a 1957 model all dented up, but in his mind it was still good. This became the expression, "Peepaw New."

He would call his grandson about a tool or a piece of clothing, and promise that it was brand new. My son would come home grinning and shaking his head over a worn-out tool or a threadbare jacket that was "Peepaw New."

Peepaw passed away last year, but we still use "Peepaw New" in our family, and we just smile because we all know what it means.

What Will People Think?

CHRIS HEETER

Marcia was visiting her mother at the Alzheimer's wing in a nursing home. It had been a hard decision to move her to the nursing home, but things were actually going quite well. Her mother enjoyed the company of the other residents, and, in fact, had decided that she was running the dining room. No one dissuaded her from her idea.

Although her mother had lost much of her ability to remember things, she had not lost her spunk and cleverness. Once when Marcia was helping her in the bathroom, she discovered her mother was wearing seven pairs of underwear. When asked about this, her mother got a twinkle in her eyes and said, "People take these, you know."

Marcia was an upstanding citizen and minister in her upper-middle-class suburb. It was a community that did not allow a lot of room for differences. She often found this unsettling, but managed to both fit in and be herself most of the time.

On one of her visits with her mother, Marcia walked in nicely dressed and wearing new red loafers. Her mother noticed them instantly, and commented on how beautiful they were. After the third comment on her shoes, Marcia suggested that her mother try them on, and if she liked them, Marcia would buy her a pair in her size.

Her mother tried on the red shoes, and shuffled around exclaiming how much she liked them. The shoes were so large on her, you could see the gap between her heel and the end of the shoe. Marcia agreed the shoes looked nice on her, and offered again to pick up a pair for her in her size, and bring them to her next time.

Her mother said again, "I really like *this pair* of shoes!"

Marcia understood, saying, "You really like this pair, don't you?"

Her mother beamed.

Marcia had to make a decision, but quickly started to have concerns. What would the nurses think if I gave my mother a pair of shoes that fit her so badly? I would have to walk out in my stockings, and it is wintertime, and people might think I was a patient rather than a visitor here. Maybe I should be stricter with my mother.

The thoughts competed in her head, but she knew what she had to do.

"Mom, you look beautiful," she said as she gave her a hug goodbye. Then she walked out of that nursing home—stocking-footed, and with her head held high.

Wheelchair Soup

BRENDA ELSAGHER

Dad was always creative when it came to cooking, spicing meats up for the grill, or throwing some interesting soup together in his huge stock pot.

The last couple of years of my father's life, he was restricted to a wheelchair, but that didn't change his "creative cooking." The only difference was that now, when he cleaned out the refrigerator to find wilted veggies and some hunk of meat, the soup was always referred to as wheelchair soup. Whatever he could reach from his wheelchair went into the soup. After he peeled and cut everything, he'd add various spices into the pot and ultimately, it always tasted pretty good. One day I stopped over just as he was serving the "wheelchair soup." We were chatting away when I looked on my soup spoon and found a rubber band.

"Look what I found in my soup, Dad," I said, tilting my spoon forward so he could see the rubber band.

Without missing a beat, he said, "Well, I didn't know how many were coming over; I had to find a way to stretch out the soup!"

The Mexican Hat Dance

SHERRY WENBORG

On my grandmother's eighty-second birthday, we went to visit her in the nursing home. The whole family was there, three kids and four adults. She had a roommate sitting nearby in her wheelchair. My grandmother was opening her gifts, and we were eating cake and singing happy birthday, all enjoying our visit.

We had been there about an hour when my aunt noticed a puddle of urine on the floor underneath the roommate's wheelchair when she moved her chair. In a loving effort to save face for the roommate, my aunt left the room for a moment. She didn't say anything to anybody when she slipped into the bathroom during the celebration, and came out with several towels. She promptly threw the towels on the floor covering the puddle, and with a loud, fun voice, she said, 'Who knows the Mexican hat dance?" With elaborate choreography, she threw her arms in the air, and began clapping her hands, and jumping on the towels while making a lot of fun noise, prompting everyone to get into the spirit of the moment.

We were all entertained by her whimsical display. She was quite a fun-loving character, so it wasn't out of line for her to do that. She was very creative and intelligent, and that day I recognized how compassionate she was too. With a glorious sweeping motion at the end, she picked up the towels and threw them into the bathtub. To this day, whenever I hear the Mexican hat dance, I remember my aunt fondly, and I smile.

Scarred for Life

BRENDA ELSAGHER

One morning at the breakfast table when my kids were in junior high, they got into the subject of scars on their bodies. Both of them, being rambunctious in their youth, had a couple to show off.

"See this one, Mom? This is when the neighbor boys threw the rock that hit me on the chin!"

"Oh, yes, I remember. It was so sad when Dad was carrying you back home."

"Look at this one," my daughter said. "I still have a scar from my broken arm when I was five."

Not wanting to miss out on participating, I thought I'd raise my shirt to show them the really impressive scar on my abdomen. Not thinking about it, I lifted my shirt upwards to show my tummy.

"You guys want to see something really impressive?" As I lifted my shirt, they both got horrified looks.

"Mom, you don't have your bra on!" It must have been traumatic to see what gravity can do. They didn't even notice the long scar on my tummy.

Then my son said, "I could live the rest of my life without ever seeing that again!"

"Well, son, you weren't complaining when you were nursing from them!"

He rolled his eyes and kept eating.

Swimming with the Snarks

MAXINE JEFFRIS

So, you like to think your memory is still pretty good, eh? Well then, don't hang out with your adult children. All you have to do is introduce one son by his brother's name, and suddenly you're "losing it." Use his sister's name, and they're packing your bags for the nearest memory-care facility.

Certainly I have my share of "senior moments," but what's new? Even as a high school senior, I often failed to remember that Monday was a school day. And still I graduated, so what does that tell us? It tells us that education and a good memory are way overrated. And don't forget it.

So what if I wasn't valedictorian (had to use spell check for that one). Nobody I hung out with wanted to be accused of being "so smart." Aspiring valedictorians hung out in the library with their noses in a book, while the rest of us hung out in the parking lot with our noses in a beer. The cool choice was obvious.

However, I was not at the very bottom of my class, for that position belonged to "Danny De Comatose" for four, actually five, unchallenged years. My brief fling with Danny (he had wheels) lasted until about half an hour after his dad took away what was left of his '57 Chevy Belair, and replaced it with a three-speed Schwinn. Not enough wheels for me. The idea of his fuzzy dice hanging from his handlebars helped me move on.

I think my brilliant snark meisters go after my soft under-belly (from which I brought them forth, and where's the thanks for that?) out of revenge. They are taking nips for all the times I answered their incessant childish questions with "I don't know."

Though my children may be sparkly bright now, they never asked the truly interesting questions like, "Where do babies come from?" Oh, how I could have gone on and on about that. I love talking about where babies come from. But no, they asked questions like, "Why does Jello jiggle?" Well, first off, I did not want to get into the ugly facts of gelatin and cow hooves, as my kids would have scrunched up their faces and refused to accept Jello as a delicious, nutritious dessert ever again. Second, if I did bother to explain things, they would glaze over after two sentences, and start picking at their scabs.

Along with lots of Jello, my kids thrived (the really cute kids stay small) on Spaghetti O's, Oreos, and Cheerios. If it didn't roll, they wouldn't eat it. One day my son ate all the wheels from a Matchbox car. We never did find them.

Now they eat all kinds of creepy stuff: brains, snails, ground-up liver. Yuck. They probably drink the water from old flower arrangements for the nutrients.

But I digress.

I still regard "I don't know" as an acceptable response to questions from anyone under the age of twenty, and contend that I don't deserve punishment for having been succinct. BTW: for grandchildren, "Google it" gets the job done without wasting time explaining ear hair.

I freely write all this because younger folk these days do not read anything that's bogged down with whole words correctly spelled, u no? Therefore, I am safe in revealing that I have a new default response: "I did not!" which is super-handy for those ugly trips down memory lane. When, for instance, the kids nip at me for the time I forgot to pick them up from camp camp was for only one measly week? Who knew! I look them squarely in the chin, and emphatically state, "I did not!" Try it, they'll back off. In my case, they blame it on all that beer.

Advice from a Nine-Year-Old

BRENDA ELSAGHER

When I was forty-two years old, I finally enrolled in college. It was always a goal of mine to attend college; I was just waiting until I knew what I wanted to be when I grew up. Someone along the way told me it wasn't necessary to pick a major just yet—get the generals done, and then perhaps I would figure it out. I had owned my own business for twenty years, and wanted to stretch myself into something besides business.

After taking the assessments to determine my capabilities, I found out that even though I scored high in the writing portion, my algebra needed help. I thought I would get my least-interesting class over first, so I plunged into the dark abyss of math. I used math daily in business, and my husband assured me I used algebra all the time when I measured, calculated, and doubled recipes at home. When placing furniture in a room with space restrictions or comparing ounces and costs at the grocery store, I used algebra. Paying bills and making calculations in my checkbook were other practical uses. I applied it practically, so why not academically? It was good to know, but I doubt I would ever be a math teacher. At least I could teach my kids how to make banana bread. Both skills are important, so why was I so freaked out?

I got excited about algebra and understood it in class, but

when I got home again, nothing I had learned made sense on paper. I was pounding on the table out of frustration, trying to make my scientific calculator do the described problem, and plugging in the information was not yielding the desired results. I had struggled with equations and my homework for two hours when I overheard my nine-year-old son tell his sister in a quiet voice, "Look at Mom. She can't figure out her math problems in college. That is why we are going to go to college right away after high school. We don't want to be old like her."

A Story with Teeth in It

BOB RAMSEY

The coming and going of teeth seems to accompany certain milestones in both growing up and growing older. For example, teething marks the demarcation point between "babyness" and true infancy. Likewise, the loss of "baby teeth" around age five to seven is linked with the commencement of formal education. And at the other end of the aging spectrum, the loss of teeth announces the onset of "elderness."

In my family, we have a running joke that you know you are old when you have to get up in the middle of the night and put on your glasses to find your teeth, so you can chew some Rolaids to ease your heartburn.

Teeth (or their absence) signify benchmarks in the aging process. After all, there's a reason we refer to old people as "long in the tooth," and why "toothless" and "hag" go together. Teeth tell a tale.

That must be why I have vivid tooth memories. I recall the first time my mother pulled one of my loose teeth by tying a thread around it and jerking away. Not long after, I found a windfall under my pillow, compliments of a magnanimous Tooth Fairy. It was only a dime, however this was a bonanza to a little kid in the 1940s.

And I remember breaking off a front tooth when I was in

the third grade, and having it replaced by one twice its size. This tooth just hung there in my mouth for years until the rest of my teeth caught up with it.

I also recall numerous fear-filled visits to the dentist, and suffering the agony of de-teeth at the hands of a sadistic dental hygienist.

Years later, my kindly old oral surgeon said, "You're going to love my drugs." I woke later to find five or six more teeth missing—but no swelling, bruising, bleeding, or pain. (Bless you, Doc.) However, this happened again and again, until I had no more teeth left.

My most memorable teeth event occurred when my youngest grandson, Adam, came running up to me one day proudly announcing, "Look, Grandpa, I lost a tooth," and held it out for my inspection and admiration. Yes, I should have expressed wonder at such a momentous event, praised him for his marvelous accomplishment, and shut my mouth.

Instead, I puffed myself up and said, "That's nothing. See what I can do." Then I popped out my full set of dentures and handed them to him. It's true, we're never too old to be a smart aleck.

My grandson was speechless! Stunned! Awestruck! His face reflected total wonder and disbelief. I retrieved my teeth, feeling pleased with myself, and thought it ended there. I was wrong.

The next day when my wife and I went to pick up our grandson from daycare, I quickly discovered I had become famous overnight. Upon entering the daycare center, I was immediately mobbed by preschool groupies yelling, "Adam's grandpa, show us your teeth." Under pressure, however, I remained tight-lipped, and the furor eventually subsided.

A few days after I had survived the munchkin mob scene,

my grandson asked if he could take me to school for "show and tell." Yikes!

Thankfully, after considerable discussion, I convinced him that personal tooth talk should remain in the family. My fame was short-lived, but the memory lingers. The entire oral episode is etched indelibly in my mind—and in my grandson's mind—and, perhaps, in the minds of a whole generation of preschool alumni.

Now I keep my dentured mouth shut around little kids and dental hygienists. Even though I learned this life lesson too late, those with grandkids and false teeth can benefit from my hard-earned wisdom in time to avoid similar embarrassment. Remember, "What happens in the mouth stays in the mouth."

The Casket

Brenda Elsagher

My mom and dad were very kind to us children when they pre-planned their funeral arrangements. They paid for their plots, coffins, and even their obituaries.

Dad was telling us how the meeting went, and had some encouraging news.

"Well, the undertaker came over today and talked about our wishes for our funerals, caskets and all. She was here for quite a while discussing the things we wanted. I told her I wanted to be cremated, and she was kind of surprised."

She said, "Usually people of your generation don't want to be cremated. Do you mind if I ask why you would rather have that than be buried in a casket?"

He had always been a very large man. (Just imagine your refrigerator, put a smile on it, and that was my dad.) A big hunk of a loveable man. He said, "All my life I've had to pay extra for big-sized clothes, larger furniture, a bigger car, and I don't want to pay extra for a super-sized casket when I can just get cremated, and one person can carry me instead of eight."

She smiled at him and said, "Well, I will talk to my boss to find out if there would be an extra charge for your casket, but I doubt it. You should be able to fit."

"Well, I don't want to be squished into it, like my head

having to be placed off kilter so I can squeeze in. I already have to do that with my car simply to get in. That would not look good," he said with a laugh.

"I'll get back to you on this later on today when I get back to the office."

She called him in the afternoon. "I have good news! You can be buried in the casket without worrying about your head being squished, you will fit."

He retorted, "I've got another question for you. If I get sick at the end, and lose a lot of weight, could I get a discount?" They both laughed and turned an unusual and sometimes difficult conversation into one of many funny stories we have enjoyed telling about our dad.

Grandparents and Car Seats

CAROL LARSON

Our son-in-law, Matt, had to go to Savannah, Georgia, for the work week. My husband, Dave, and I jumped at the opportunity to have our daughter, Jenn, and their children stay at our house for two nights. Jenn has a full-time marketing job, and all we had to do was drive our one-year-old grandson, Brett, and our three-year-old granddaughter, Josie, to separate daycare facilities.

On Monday, Dave picked up Matt at 7 a.m. and drove him to the airport. Jenn took the children to daycare in the morning, and that afternoon, brought the children to our house and set up the car seats in our car for the next day. Dave picked up a nutritious fast-food meal, and after putting the children to bed, Jenn and I watched TV.

The real fun began Tuesday morning when Jenn left for work at 7:45 a.m. Josie woke up at 8:15 in tears because her mother had already gone. We put on cartoons, made toaster waffles, and everyone settled down. About 9 a.m., we began the task of putting on their jackets, mittens, and hats, which took us about a half hour. We had Josie's "baba," her "blankie," Brett's "blankie," and Brett's bottles and diapers. We even understood what these words meant. Pretty good, we thought.

We had the foresight to warm our car as the temperature was

now close to zero. However, Brett's car seat did not fit into the base as it was supposed to. Dave struggled with it for almost fifteen minutes until the cold brought him into the house. Finally, he loosely placed it on top, and tied the car seat belt around Brett's waist and the adult seat belt over the whole contraption. Now it was my turn. Josie's car seat fit neatly, but the seat belt was a conundrum. I guess I was supposed to figure out how to fasten the darn seat belt because I am good at solving puzzles. Apparently not the steel ones that have two tops that latch on to one another, if you know what to do, then fit into the bottom thingamajig, which by now had slipped under her legs. I failed miserably. The kids just watched us with interest, stupefied. If they were worried about the competence of their grandparents, they didn't let on. We finally just tied what we could together, and decided to go. It was now 9:45. I kept looking back at the children, occasionally holding on to Brett's car seat. Josie didn't seem to mind that her car seat belt was tied, too.

I had to meet a friend for an early lunch after we left off the children. Momentarily I thought I might end up bringing the children along to lunch, but we made it to the daycare centers, and the lovely young women running the centers ran out to our car and helped our grandchildren out of the car. When we came back at 3 p.m., they politely pointed out that Brett's car seat should be facing the other way, and showed us how easily Josie's seat belt could be assembled, expertly buckling them within three minutes.

"Oh, of course," we said, still not sure we understood.

We made our way home, sent out for chow mein, and watched a DVD from Veggie Tales called *The Wizard of Pods*. Jenn and I caught just a little bit of the movie *Butch Cassidy and the Sundance Kid*. My last image of the movie was seeing Paul Newman and Robert Redford plunge from a high cliff into rapids. Our plight was not quite so dramatic, but resembled our feeling of being totally confounded because of our lack of experience. Then we fell asleep. The next morning, the house seemed empty. Jenn and the kids had left, and we did not have the same challenging tasks ahead of us to perform. But we were able to shake hands and say, "Mission accomplished!"

The Insensitivity of Kids

Brenda Elsagher

After recently having my second tooth pulled, I reflected to the time when in her late thirties my young mother was struggling with partial dentures. Totally preoccupied with my own teenage needs, I didn't even realize what she was going through as she stood ironing my shirts for school.

Her eight children were afoot, and probably annoying each other and her. She abruptly slammed her iron down on the ironing board and yelled at us. "You kids make me *tho thick*!"

In a flash, we all realized she was trying to say "so sick" and we burst out laughing.

She was demoralized and ran into her room, crying. What goes around comes around, and I am thinking of her these days as my teeth are disappearing.

Section V
Learning Adventures

"A person needs new experiences.
It jars something deep inside, allowing them to grow.
Without change something sleeps inside us, and
seldom awakens. The sleeper must awaken."

—FRANK HERBERT

Sweetheart

MARSHA WARREN MITTMAN

In my search for a new place to live over a period of two to three years, I'd visited various locales in nine different states. Nothing seemed to click. Lovely though they may be, Vermont, New Hampshire, the Carolinas, Florida, New Mexico, Montana, and California didn't speak to me. Having been widowed young, with two independent children, as well as parents who still had each other, I was, literally, a free bird for the first time in my life. But where to fly?

So there I was, checking out Denver and Fort Collins, the former too similar (albeit on a smaller scale) to my home city of New York, and the latter too similar to a New York suburb.

For the longest time, a friend who had purchased land for retirement in the Black Hills had been championing South Dakota. I knew it was out west somewhere, up there someplace. But really, South Dakota? Seriously?

Perplexed, I was standing in Denver, and I made a snap decision. I was going to visit Spearfish where my friend owns land. With no car, no maps, no GPS, no AAA triptik, no concept of where Spearfish is in relation to Denver, and absolutely no idea of where I was going, I marched myself into a bus station and asked if they go to South Dakota.

"Of course, mam."

"Spearfish?"

"Of course, mam."

Elated, I proclaimed, "Put me on the bus!"

And so the adventure began, winding our way up through Colorado and Wyoming. What the ticket attendant neglected to mention was that there was a few hours' layover in the dead of night while waiting for a bus transfer. The locale—an old bar with tufted red velvet walls and a mirrored ceiling—gave new meaning to the term layover. I certainly got an eyeful of the Wild West that night. What an experience. I never saw so much comings and goings in my life.

Having survived intact, I was absolutely thrilled with my eventual first views of Spearfish as the bus approached the small town. The area felt vibrant, and the air smelled fresh. At the end of the run the bus was empty, except for me—this lone traveler from Denver—as it pulled into a closed gas station very early on a quiet Sunday morning.

The driver, upon hauling my voluminous valise out of the belly of the bus, looked around at the deserted gas station and said, "No one's here. Who's picking you up?"

"Nobody."

"Whaddaya mean—nobody? Who's coming to get you?"

"No one," I repeated. "I don't know anybody here."

"Whaddaya mean, you don't know anyone here? Seriously, who's coming to meet you?"

"No one," I said, for the third time. And as the driver looked at me incredulously, I explained I'd come to check the area out, without knowing anyone in town.

"Don't worry about me," I quickly assured him. "I'll get a taxi."

"Sweetheart, there are no taxis here."

"I'll rent a car."

Eyes rolling, hands on hips, the driver hit me with, "Sweetheart, there are no rental agencies here."

I could just hear his brain registering crazy city chick.

"Not to worry. It's a small town. I'll walk to the nearest motel, and figure it out from there."

"Sweetheart," he said again, as his eyes drop to my bare feet in my strappy high-heeled city-style summer sandals standing next to the huge valise, "You're not gonna make it two blocks in those shoes with that valise; the closest motel is two miles. You sure you don't know anyone here?"

"Not a soul."

Big sigh, a pause, and then he threw my valise back under the bus. I assumed he was going to drive me to the nearest motel.

He announced, "Sweetheart, get back in the bus. I'll take you to a car rental."

I protested, but he insisted, and off we went, presumably to the next town to a car rental agency. What I didn't know was that this angel of a man at the end of his long run, finished with work on a beautiful Sunday morning, intended to drive me to Rapid City's airport an hour away. It was the only place in South Dakota west river territory where an impetuous crazy city chick could rent a car. And then he first had to drive an hour back to Spearfish where he lived.

On the way to the airport, I sat up front next to him on the bus, listening to his stories about South Dakota.

"Born and bred, my dad too. Grandad came over from the old country, bought some land and started farming, and that was that. Got two kids of my own. South Dakota's been home for four generations now."

At the airport, he once again hauled my valise out of the bus's belly after pointing me in the direction of the rental car locations. I offered him $50 for his time and courtesy, and I was shocked when he refused the money.

"Sweetheart," he smiled as he shook my proffered hand, "glad to have been able to help," he said, and off he went.

My decision was made at that moment. I would move to Spearfish, South Dakota. From the beauty I had seen, the fresh air and good vibes I felt, and the kindness I'd experienced, there seemed to be something very special in the area—something I'd been searching for, but until then, hadn't found.

This past year I learned that all my relatives back east, when they heard I had moved to Spearfish from a population of ten million people to ten thousand, took bets on how fast I'd return to New York City. One month, three months, six months, they guessed. One even bet I'd give it a try for a year.

It's actually going on sixteen years, and all my relatives back in New York now refer to me as that crazy country chick. The real sweetheart of this story was without a doubt the bus driver, who wouldn't let a crazy city chick get stranded.

Automated Tollbooth Battle

Brian R. Lee

One of the greatest experiences of growing up in the Baby Boomer generation is that we got to watch technology expand at a wondrous rate around us. But we also often discovered that the older we got, the harder it was to keep up with that expansion. The most difficult times were when it would blindside us in what we expected to be a normal, minor task of life.

A couple years back, I was driving to Upstate New York to see my son. As I went through Indiana, I found the tollbooths were devoid of humans—they'd been automated. Starting out, it wasn't so bad; I just took the ticket that stuck out of the machine like an accusing finger. It was similar to the entrances of many pay-for-parking lots.

But then it came time to pay the money. I was sitting behind a car, wondering what was taking him so long, until finally it was my turn. I inserted my ticket in the clearly marked slot, when it spit it out. I tried again, and it spit it out again. I turned it around, placed it upside down, but the machine clearly did not like the taste of this ticket. After a few times, my patience dissipated, and took with it my gentleness. I shoved the ticket as deeply in the slot as I could, and held my hand over the slot so it couldn't come back out. Apparently this piece of technology likes it rough. The price I'm supposed to pay, along with the number of axles I'm being charged for, was finally displayed on a screen. What? It wants $48 for seven axles? I'm driving a little Mazda, for crying out loud.

When I pushed the button for "help," a recording told me all the agents were busy, and I would receive assistance when my turn came up in the queue. I glanced in my rearview mirror, and noticed cars were starting to back up behind me. Finally someone answered, and when I told him the problem, he quickly corrected it to the proper $4 toll. Apparently he's had to fix this problem before—perhaps often.

So, I started pushing dollar bills in the slot. The first one was rejected, so I tried another one. The second one went in, but the third, fourth, and fifth were rejected. After going through a dozen singles, I ran out, so I started asking my passengers for dollar bills. Pretty soon I had rejected dollar bills laying all over my lap and the floor of the car until we finally found four bills good enough for the machine. I let out a cheer as the gate opened—apparently the only part of that contraption working properly.

I've never been so happy to leave a state. It was as if the Berlin Wall separating Indiana from Ohio had fallen. This automated system was so bad that when I got to the next toll-booth in Ohio and saw a human there as I pulled up, I said to her with longing eyes, "I love you." And she knew exactly what I meant.

Traveling with "the Kids"

BRENDA ELSAGHER

Before my husband, Bahgat, and I were married, we traveled to San Francisco with our friends Pat and Tom. Bahgat decided to be the designated driver for the entire trip, and we loved that. We got into a routine of the two of us in the front seat, and Pat and Tom in the back. Bahgat started calling them kids on the trip, and we were all pushing thirty at the time.

"Where shall I drive you kids next?" was a common question before we headed off toward our next destination.

We arrived at the Exploratorium in San Francisco, and my husband did his usual joking. As we arrived to the entrance to pay admission, my husband said, "Two adults and two kids, please."

Without hesitation, the cashier said, "Well, I don't believe those are your children, but I do believe you two are senior citizens."

He gave us the discount, and we happily went on our way.

To Become Un-Invisible

KAY CASKEY AND LAURIE YOUNG

Our kids were launched and out of college. We finally had more time and money for some long-awaited adventures. Our philosophy has always been, "Do whatever you are capable of doing today, because you may not be able to do it tomorrow." And it wouldn't hurt to show the kids what we were made of since we were pretty much invisible to them, and hopelessly uncool.

Climbing Mt. Kilimanjaro seemed to fit the bill. Except maybe we weren't capable of doing it. Perhaps our time had passed, and we were already at tomorrow. We had been runners, but hiking to over nineteen thousand feet? No, we'd never done something that challenging. This was the big one for us and we trained, as much as you can train climbing on southwest Michigan's one-and-only ski slope, called Mt. Baker.

A friend, having already topped Mt. Baker, had dreamed of climbing Kilimanjaro. This was a true mountain climb, not a trek, with self-arrests and ice axes while tied to the leader with ropes. We warned her we were long-haul, slow-footed types, but she was game, and joined the expedition. We called the tour company to see if others would be joining us.

"Yes, there was one more. A woman. Oh, and she's from your state, Michigan!"

She was from just ninety miles away on the other side of

the state.

Thoughts intruded.

"Please tell us she isn't thirty-two years old," we pleaded.

The tour operator was taken aback, not really understanding, saying, "Looks like she's in her fifties."

Relief washed over us.

"Oh, good."

Our Tanzanian guide, Eric, said the plan was to go "pole, pole" (pronounced pole-ay, pole-ay), Swahili for "slowly, slowly." He had made over two hundred ascents, but had never guided an all-woman team and never one so . . . well . . . old. But he was undaunted, or at least hid any apprehension he might have felt, even though only about 50 percent of the people who attempt the climb make it to the summit.

The guides were excellent and took great care of us. They called us bibis, a name we thought they might bestow on all their clients. A few days into the climb we learned Eric was taking some teasing from the other guides about us. Our age averaged fifty-seven, and we were no one's idea of perfect clients. Under some pressure, he admitted bets were being made, and lotteries set up to predict whether we would make it, or more accurately, at what altitude we would give up. He said he thought we would go all the way, but we never learned how much money he was willing to put down on that prediction.

Our guide was probably just as happy as we were when all four of us made it to the top of the world. We learned later, to our chagrin, that bibi doesn't mean babes, but grandmothers.

Our kids congratulated us, but seemed blasé about what we thought was an incredible accomplishment, confirmed by guides from around the mountain.

A few years later, we signed up for an adventure tour of New Zealand, the country famous for creating all kinds of crazy stunt tricks, including the world's first bungee jump. What would cause someone to imagine that would be a fun activity?

Queenstown really is the adventure capital of the world, with every possible escapade available. We could select from an endless array of crazy activities, from kayaking to parachuting to horseback riding. Kay's son had advised us to choose something on the "sweet side of danger," so our guide suggested the Luge Ride, little sliding go-carts with clutch brakes you can pull when your speed gets uncomfortable (the sour side of danger?).

We donned our helmets and slipped behind the controls, along with several ten-year-old boys, and then veered down the mountain. When we got to the bottom unscathed, we looked at each other with some surprise, and said almost in unison, "I wasn't scared at all."

The day was still new so we looked around for other alternatives. The Queenstown Mountain sports one of the longest zip lines in the world. We decided to go for it. It had several on-off ramps, and as we headed down, they tried to jack up the fear factor, and we ended up flying upside down through the pine trees, traces of the ski trails still visible beneath the summer grass below. When we arrived at the bottom, we looked at each other and knew—it looked a lot scarier than it really was. So we weren't sure how we would weave this into a great story for our time on the sweet spot of danger.

When we headed down, we saw on the other side of the mountain people were riding the wind on paraglides—large kites with people hanging from harnesses. When we first arrived we saw people going down in tandem with a guide. We knew we could never do such a thing. No, that would really be crazy. Not going to happen. But then, maybe we could just go watch.

They looked like competent young men. Even so, Kay began

to question them vigorously. "How many times have you done this? Ever seen any accidents? What is your relationship with your grandmother? Any death wishes? Are you suicidal at all? Are you depressed?"

We decided to go for it. Wow, this thrilling adventure might finally be it. The ride was spectacular. What a view—and the landing perfect. We weren't scared at all, and we really had something to show our kids. It had been a very full day.

We rejoined the tour, and shared our stories. The van headed out of Queenstown, but the guide had one more spot for us to see.

He explained, "The very first bungee jump was done right here in Queenstown."

One of our co-travelers, a marine and his new wife, decided they would take the plunge. We looked at each other. No, never. But then here we were. Could we? We went up to inquire, and before we knew it, we had our weight prominently written on our hands, and we were ushered up to the plunge platform.

"Do you want a wet (wet, as in your head goes into the water) or a dry jump?" asked Steve, our bungee leader.

"Dry!" said Kay. "We want a conservative bungee jump."

Steve looked at her and said, "Why are you here?"

We were strapped up together—many go in tandem, so if one goes, the other goes with them. This was really crazy. Oh. My. God. It was so far down there. What the heck were we doing, and why? Definitely not the sweet spot. We were way past that marker.

We feel a small nudge from the back, and off we go.

A little yellow rubber dingy on the river was waiting to fetch the plungers off their ropes, or out of the river if they chose a "wet" ride. As the men hauled us into the boat, one looked down at us with a look of horror and said, "How old are you?"

But we were redeemed. As we climbed up the ramp to rejoin our group, the way was lined with elderly Korean tourists who had postponed their bus departure to see if we would really do it. We felt like Angie and Brad as we heard applause and cameras clicking.

We finally did impress the kids, but what really caught their notice, what finally got us into the "cool" category, was something that demanded not a bit of fitness or adrenaline bravery. We both love humor, so we elected to have a two-inch design of the Groucho Marx kind of typical mustache, big round glasses, and a big nose with bushy eyebrows, tattooed on our hips.

Of all the adventures we did, this is the one that got us noticed, and at last, we were visible to our kids again.

The Pyramids

Bahgat Elsagher

My uncle in Egypt was sixty-four when he was told he had only a short time left to live.

I asked him, "What is it that you haven't done that you would like to do before you leave this life?"

Much to my surprise he said, "I would like to see the pyramids."

I knew he lived only forty miles away from them, and I was shocked to learn he had never been there.

The next morning, I picked him up and made the ninety-minute journey past the countryside, into the city and the tourist area of the Great Pyramids of Giza. I watched his face as he looked at the pyramids, and then drove around to the other side so he could see the famous Sphinx as well.

Not seeming too impressed, he said sarcastically, "This is what people are coming from all over the world to see? A bunch of giant structures?"

He had thought he would see some kind of a fantastic show with dancing and music, some form of entertainment. Since he could not physically go into the pyramids, or walk around the Sphinx, we went to a local coffee shop where he enjoyed watching the tourists. He was more fascinated by the people from different cultures and their unique looks. He had never seen anyone but Egyptians, and this was the first time he saw Asian people. He was much more impressed by them.

When we returned, he told his family about the amazing variety of people he saw, which was more exciting for him than the pyramids. I was glad I could bring him to a new adventure at that time in his life. He died a few days later.

The Joss Sticks

MARSHA WARREN MITTMAN

We'd hired a guide to go upriver. We loved traveling on our own, to places not frequented by tourists. And so we set out early one morning to see Thailand's hill tribes—those not close to Bangkok, and weren't visited by ubiquitous bus tours. These tribes were accessible by river only, having no interior roads. Our longboat was a narrow, charred, hollowed-out tree half with a balustrade and two little benches in the middle, poled by a lone oarsman.

We spent a few hours on the river, my husband dozing during most of the trip. We passed by the more commercial villages located close to the city. Tribeswomen standing shoreline beckoned us to buy wares displayed on makeshift racks at the water's edge. Naked toddlers ran free in the sand. Dogs raced along the shore barking at us. Occasionally we'd catch sight of a crocodile slithering out of the water.

And then settlements started to dwindle, eventually disappearing altogether. Just as I started getting a bit nervous—no one knew where we'd gone—our guide gestured for the oarsman to dock. As we rounded a curve in the river, we were stunned to find ourselves facing a magnificent, ancient Buddhist temple complex.

The guide advised us to disembark and use the "facilities"

since these would be the last available for a while. A few monks in residence subsequently gave us a brief tour, and then suggested we throw the "joss sticks," saying they would bring us good fortune.

I was handed a tall, worn cylindrical container in which numerous long, numbered, thin reeds had been placed. I was told to hold the container at a forty-five-degree angle and gently shake it, until one stick dislodged itself from the others and fell to the ground. The guide would then take this stick to the temple's resident Master, a "seer," and for a donation we would be told what the future held for us according to the selected providential joss stick.

"Yeah, right. Clever way," I thought, "to get the occasional tourist to help with the temple's upkeep." However, the temple badly needed care, and these people were palpably poor. So I decided to play the game.

A monk said a prayer over the container. I paid homage to Buddha as best I could since this was my initial contact with him, and then I was instructed to kneel on the floor and shake the container in front of me. Not as easy as it sounds—the sticks flew all over the place. A very careful second attempt elicited a lone stick, which was ceremoniously carried to the seer. After deliberation, our guide carried a message back to me.

"Master says you have recently planted seeds that with careful watering and cultivation will blossom into beautiful flowers." The guide beamed. "What," he demanded to know, "have you recently started doing that could change your life so serendipitously?"

I thought and thought, but the only thing I could come up with was the fact that I had started meditating a number of months before; otherwise everything else in my life was status quo. Surprised at my answer, the guide carried the message back to the seer who, of course, as a Buddhist, advised me to continue meditating.

This is a hoot, I thought, as I handed my husband the container. He managed to single out one stick on his first try, and we were laughing and kidding about the "game" as our guide once again headed to the seer. We stopped laughing upon his return for he was very subdued. He said the message wasn't clear, and my husband needed to throw the sticks again. He carried my husband's second stick to the seer. But when he returned, again he relayed no message.

When I pressed him for an answer, he simply said, "On occasion the sticks don't work. Master sends his humble apologies."

We left our donations. The monks walked us back to their tiny pier, and watched us depart. We continued our trip upriver to the first of three villages we were to see that day. They were amazing and well worth the long river trip.

On our return to Bangkok that evening, as my husband dozed again, our guide motioned me to the front of the boat. We spoke quietly so as not to create a disturbance.

I was shocked when he suddenly asked, "Is your husband ill?"

Yes, my husband was ill. He'd been diagnosed a couple years earlier with adult-onset diabetes. He was in denial, had always enjoyed perfect health, and though affiliated with the medical field himself, had refused treatment. On the rare occasion when he paid attention to the disease, he self-medicated. Neither entreaties nor logic helped, and he wouldn't discuss his illness with anyone—which is why I started to meditate. The stress of dealing with his illness and denial had begun to take a toll on me.

So there I was in a longboat on a river in Thailand, most

unexpectedly explaining the situation to my guide, who looked very concerned, and suddenly it hit me.

"The joss stick," I said. "The Master indicated he's going to die, right?"

The answer was yes. And the seer had instructed the guide to tell me so I would be prepared. Suddenly our chance experience at the temple didn't seem like much of a game.

"How much time do we have?" I asked the guide.

"One year," he replied.

This encounter was never mentioned to anyone. Our trip continued as planned, we lived our lives as usual. I didn't believe in psychics, and had never visited one. During the ensuing year I would occasionally think of the seer's warning, especially when my husband's energy seemed sapped, or he'd suffer mood swings due to sugar aberrations. But life just seemed to roll on.

We had visited the Buddhist temple the first week in December. I said a silent prayer when the following December closed a year later—the year had come and gone with no mishap. So much for the seer's warning.

The following month, mid-January, while we were dancing at a wedding, my husband had a massive heart attack. He died instantly, right there on the dance floor. Five doctors attending the affair were unable to resuscitate him. I stood by in shock, not only from his death, but from the realization that the seer had been correct, had actually been able to foretell the future. My logical brain screamed, "How was this possible?"

Not only that, but as if to hammer the point home that there is "more" than what our logically trained western minds can see and know, it's as if the actual timing and scenario of my husband's death had been "tweaked." There were so many "coincidences" that "chance" seemed impossible. It almost felt like the old Buddhist Master was looking over my shoulder trying to make a point, trying to get something through my thick skull.

Our son had been working in Hong Kong, thus we hadn't seen him in a year. But he'd returned home to attend the wedding and so, before he died, my husband spent time with our son. The wedding was on my husband's side of the family. He died late in the evening, and that day, he had seen all his favorite relatives. My husband enjoyed dressing up. The wedding was black tie, and he passed away in style in a spanking-new tuxedo. A lover of good food and sweets, he'd just finished a fabulous dinner replete with a decadent dessert buffet. A caring man, he died at the very end of the wedding, so he didn't put a pall on the entire evening. Most important, he absolutely loved to dance, which is what he was doing at the time of his death, so he was happy when he died. His heart attack occurred while doing a "lindy," his favorite dance style. And we just happened to be doing the lindy to his favorite song, "Chattanooga Choo Choo," whose last line, by the way, is ". . . won't you carry me home . . ."

Over the years this thick, western skull has continued meditating as per the Master's suggestion. Indeed, absolutely beautiful flowers have grown from the practice, as he predicted. There is more than what our logically trained minds have been taught to perceive, and meditation is the path to this greater awareness and understanding. The real beauty of this is that it's available to everyone who takes the time to plant and nourish the seeds.

As for my husband, well, he and I are occasionally in touch these days. And we're both doing just fine, thank you.

The Challenge

BRENDA ELSAGHER

I was on a plane coming home from the East Coast. I noticed the distinguished-looking gentleman next to me was speeding through the *New York Times* newspaper crossword puzzles one right after another. I felt kind of sheepish when I realized I was reading a *People* magazine. We had some polite chitchat, and he told me he taught statistics at Yale.

I teased him a little. "Kind of a brainiac, huh? I noticed you were going through those *New York Times* crossword puzzles pretty easily."

Modestly he said, "Some are more challenging than others."

"Are you up for a real challenge? Here's the *People* magazine Puzzler crossword. Think you can handle it?" I asked with a smile. "You only have five minutes to complete it. I am timing you now." I made a show of looking at my watch.

"Oh, this might be very difficult for me. I may not be up on my current affairs, but I'll give it a try."

"Okay, go!" I said as I whistled the *Jeopardy* tune as the minutes passed by.

"You have three minutes left!"

He finished it two minutes later, saying, "I was worried about that one."

"I'm proud of you," I told him. He beamed like a young boy.

Early Retirement

PAMELA GOLDSTEIN

My retirement started a lot like a belly flop: it seemed like a good idea at the start, but the minute it hit, I knew something was wrong. Here was the problem. As a nurse for twenty years, I was used to noise and chaos. My kids had graduated and were working in their professional fields, and our dog had just died. Nothing in my quiet home offered a sense of purpose or excitement. At first, I searched for activities to fill my days. I cleaned my house. I cleaned my house again. Went to the basement and then sterilized the entire area with an antibacterial soap. Then I cleaned shelves, the pantry, the garage, closets, drawers, even the shed in our backyard.

That took six days. What to do with the rest of my life?

Day seven: I decided that my house wouldn't really be clean unless I rearranged the furniture. I rearranged the furniture, which sucks. I decided I didn't like the furniture. Who bought that furniture in the first place? So, I bought new furniture.

The house still didn't seem clean. I painted the walls, and then I got depressed. Staying at home sucked more than rearranging furniture.

I went out to lunch with my girlfriends who told me I had rearranged the furniture wrong. When I asked when it became a science, they started quoting magazines and Martha Stewart.

I no longer liked my friends. I needed new friends. Who picked these friends anyway? After thinking about it, I decided to keep my friends, but I wouldn't have lunch with them.

I went back to my house. It still wasn't clean. Maybe it was the house. I never wanted this house. I wanted to be overlooking the water.

It was about this time that my husband, William, noted my depression. He's always been very perceptive and tactful when it comes to these things.

"What's with you? And where did we get all this furniture? And why does the house smell like a hospital?"

I muttered, "It's antibacterial soap."

"The ER smelled exactly like this and formaldehyde."

"Dinner's ready," I replied.

After a few minutes of silence, my husband put down his fork. "Okay, clearly you are not handling retirement well. You need to find some hobbies. What do your friends do, you know, the ones who have never worked?"

I smiled sweetly. "Are you talking about the ones who go to the gym every day, for hours at a time, and are on a perpetual diet, or are you thinking of the ones who go shopping every day?"

William grimaced. "Okay, so not those friends. How about Chris? She reads and . . . what does she do?"

"Walks fifteen kilometers a day with her dog, and goes grocery shopping for dinner. She spends over an hour in the veggie department alone. Our dog died. And I am not spending hours in a grocery store, every day, and planning dinner. My name is not Martha."

The next day William came home from work with a big grin, carrying a package. He handed it to me. "Open it."

It was a digital camera. "It's lovely, but—"

"We're going to Hawaii! You're depressed, and I need a break, and you've always wanted to travel and go snorkeling with those exotic fish you love—it's a perfect time to go."

"You hate to travel."

"I'll get used to it."

Two weeks later, I found myself floating near the shore in Waikiki with William by my side. Hawaii was fabulous and exciting. It smelled clean and not antibacterial. The water was warm, the weather was warm, and—

"Will," I cried. "There's a fish in my swimsuit!"

After he stopped laughing, Will went . . . um . . . fishing. "I never used to like fishing, but this is fun."

I sighed with embarrassment as he rummaged in my swimsuit, and we sunk lower in the water. "Where's murky water when you need it?"

"Got it!" he said triumphantly and pulled out a small black-and-white striped fish. "Cute little guy."

I decided my love affair with fish might be over.

Will and I have since traveled many places, and we are officially travel-holics. I spend a great deal of time taking photos and writing about my travels in journals.

One year we spent three weeks in Japan. We went on a university tour where you stayed in clean but cheaper hotels, and ate daily fare food like raw fish, rice, and miso soup. That was breakfast. Lunch got a little more interesting with the three staples of a Japanese lunch, raw fish, rice, and miso soup. Dinner, however, was always fabulous with miso soup, rice, and raw fish. Miso soup had that added favorite . . . bonito fish flakes. Again with fish.

One of the best parts of the excursion was when we arrived home. My son, Ben, a trained chef, thought he'd surprise us with a lovely dinner. He had spent hours finding the right recipes for miso soup with bonito flakes, rice, and raw fish.

Since that trip I've yet to be able to look a dead fish in the eye without cringing.

My husband has just returned from his office with that gleam in his eye. He's up to something yet again. "Honey, what do you think of Machu Picchu in January?"

"Are there any fish there?"

"I don't think they have fish. It's in the mountains."

"Oh, well, that's okay then."

I love being retired.

Hiking in Chile

KAY CASKEY AND LAURIE YOUNG

We took the shuttle ride from Puerto Natales to Torres Del Paine, a national park in Patagonia, Chile. Patagonia is pretty much at the end of the world, and the hike to the iconic Torres del Paine, those three massive slabs of granite turned on end, is considered one of the best hikes in the world—touted as *never to be forgotten.*

Looking around at all the other hikers on our shuttle bus, we noted we had at least thirty to forty years on the next youngest passenger. Hmmm, then we remembered some comments from a previous hiking companion in Mongolia who had been in Chile's park.

"The wind was horrendous. I really admire you ladies for being so adventuresome."

That night, at dinner in the lodge, a Canadian woman was counting her blessings that she could leave the following day.

"I'm never coming back here. It's the wind. Yesterday it was so fierce I could hardly stand upright. When I rounded the bend on the trail, I saw six trekkers lying flat on their backs, flailing away helplessly like upturned ticks. A wind gust had just picked them up and toppled them."

The next day the sun was shining, the wind was still, and the trail beckoned upward. Patagonia is beautiful. We had made reservations at hostels, called refugios, along the way—the first one was only three and a half hours away, according to the first sign we saw. The second sign, after hiking an hour, said the refugio was four and a half hours away. After one more hour, another sign said it was four and a half hours away. Both the wind and the sign maker appear to be capricious.

We finally reached the refugio, having lost the trail a couple of times. It was frequently muddy, blocked by tree falls, and we crossed ice-cold rushing streams, on tree trunks when they were available, barefoot when they weren't. Mostly we gritted our teeth, thought about how brave we were, and pretended not to notice the twenty-year-olds gleefully skipping on the precarious logs over the streams and hopping over the tiring deadfall.

Those twenty-year-old trekkers had arrived at tonight's refugio much earlier than we had, so there were no towels for our shower in cold water because all the hot water was also gone, and all the food was eaten except for chips. But we enjoyed a glass of wine and the amazing view.

The next day was to be a long one. It was ten miles to the next refugio, and we trekked up and down ridges, crossed abundant streams, and walked on sharp stones until finally the Torres del Paine was in view. It was definitely worth the effort. Waiting to get a photo op perched on some precarious rocks, we waited for a group of, yes twenty-year-old male trekkers, who were having contests to see who could leap the highest off the rock.

Only our acquired wisdom of our added decades kept us from informing them of their poor judgment, their loudness, and other behavior flaws. We were quite certain they might not be forever grateful for our kind, wise, and grandmotherly advice.

Now it was 3:00 p.m. and we were only halfway to our

refugio. Luckily it was midsummer, and the sun wouldn't set for hours, but we were really beginning to drag. The wind was picking up, and we were holding on to our hats. Now, only an hour from our destination, we saw four lovely Chilean women talking on a wooden walkway.

One of them leapt to her feet and with a big smile and said, "Would it be okay for you to take a photo?"

"Sure," we say, holding out our hands for her camera. "We would be happy to take your photo."

"No," she stammers, "not of us. We would like a photo of you."

"Why a photo of us?" We had never met the twenty-something women.

Then we both understood in a flash. "Because we are so old?"

She blushed, and we all started to laugh. "Yes, it is true," she said, but she didn't stop there. "It is so beautiful to see old women hiking."

Not older, old. It's a compliment, right? In the following days we had blue skies above, fabulous views, and no wind or rain. What's all this fuss about Patagonian weather? We thank our lucky stars that we are beautiful old women hiking.

Two Lanes or Four?

Brian R. Lee

Retirement provides so many more opportunities for travel. No longer restricted to "vacation time," we can make road trips as long as we want, terrorizing other motorists along the way with our senior driving habits. But it is more sporting to provide some warning, like labeling your vehicle with one of those "I'm spending my children's inheritance" bumper stickers.

I have often heard the advice that to see America, we need to get off the interstate highway system and travel the two-lane back roads. So, on a recent trip I decided to put that advice to the test and use the back roads in one direction, the Interstate on the return trip. I found that neither is really better than the other. But straying from the interstate highways will cause you to get tired of hearing "recalculating" from your GPS device.

My trip was from the Twin Cities area to an area northwest of Chicago. I used state highways down into Iowa to Dubuque, and then crossed the Mississippi River through northern Illinois. On the return trip, I took interstate 90 through Wisconsin into southern Minnesota, then turned up Minnesota 52, which is one of those roads without any real identity as to type. Highway 52 is kind of a cross between an interstate highway and a two-lane highway as it has four lanes, and stop signs govern the intersections at cross roads instead of on and off ramps. It is easy to pass slower vehicles, but also easier to hit other vehicles as they attempt to cross or pull out in front of you from a stop sign.

The weather was rainy most of the way to Illinois, which caused us to forgo stops we likely would have otherwise made. Maybe it's me, but stopping for scenic views of low-lying, monotone gray clouds, while rain pelts my head, seems to lack any appeal.

But there is something alluring about those two-lane highways meandering through the countryside. And the time spent going through the towns enjoying the charm they offered viewing the old Victorian-style houses, country churches, and quaint shops.

When you do stop, it is important to engage in a little conversation with "the locals," even if it is just to exchange pleasantries. As you would expect, often a warm feeling comes from people who know almost everyone in town, just because there are so few people there to know, and they are curious to get to know you.

And you sometimes come across unusual situations you don't experience in life in the fast lane. While stopping in the rain for fuel, our path crossed with an Amish woman pulling into the gas station in an open horse-drawn wagon. As I waited for my wife to finish powdering her nose, I held the door open for the Amish woman as she left, laden with bags of ice cream. I thought if they aren't going to drive a car to the store, they also have no freezer to store ice cream, and have to get it just before the birthday party, whatever the weather.

"Not the best day to be cruising about in a convertible," I said to her.

"Oh, well, what are you going to do," she responded with a smile under her wet bonnet. So, here I am, bummed about starting our trip in bad weather in an enclosed car, and she's smiling. There must be something about this small-town living after all. Either that, or she was anticipating eating all the delicious ice cream herself.

But friendly people aren't restricted to small towns away from the interstate highways.

While in a large antique mall just off I-90 in an area obviously designed to benefit from tourism, I was looking at a display of antique toy cars. Suddenly I found myself engaged in conversation with a man, talking about old toys and why folks are drawn to them. Soon, his wife was joining in the conversation, and then so was my wife. We spent almost as much time socializing with these strangers as we did looking at antiques. I couldn't help but think, "Who are these people?" And the interaction continued in the parking lot when we crossed paths again. These folks were so friendly, it took a while to get back on the road.

And while the two-lane roads may seem romantic, there is something to be said about being able to cut two hours off a trip because the speed limits are higher, and passing slower traffic takes much less effort and time. I also have to admit there is also less stress when we know we likely won't be getting stuck behind a slow truck on some twisting two-lane highway. I like seeing the scenery, but not the same scene forever, and there's also plenty of nice scenery along the interstate highway.

In the end, I have to say the key to experiencing the advantages of such a trip is not the shape or style of highway used. Rather, it is the mindset while traveling on those highways.

When going through a small town at thirty miles per hour, you are more apt to stop and experience what that town has to offer than when you are racing through it nonstop at sixty-five miles per hour. But if you make up your mind from the beginning to make stops wherever there is something of interest, you can experience rewards from places along the interstate just as you would along some back road.

I think as we get older, we gain more patience for slower-paced traveling. This is especially true when we're retired, and don't have to be somewhere by a specific time or date. We just have to keep in mind all along the way, either way, that half the fun of getting somewhere really can be the journey, if we stop to smell the roses along the way.

Section VI
Intimacy Fun

"I kissed my first woman and smoked my
first cigarette on the same day. I have never had time
for tobacco since."

—Arturo Toscanini

Dating Older Men

ROX TARRANT

I'm embracing my age, having turned sixty-one this year. I'm not worried about getting older; *I just don't want to become old*. I thought I would age like my mother, very graceful and elegant. I'm not. I'm aging like my father. I know this is true because I now I have hair growing out of my ears, I wear boxer shorts to bed, and I fart when I pee. I am sexy—*to no one*.

I no longer date younger men. I don't want to hear them yell out in a passionate moment, "Who's your granny?" Don't judge me because I like making love to old men, really old men. I call it boning up on history. I'm dating a lovely man now, and I call him "my old man" because he looks like Brad Pitt—from the movie *Benjamin Buttons*.

When you're dating a young guy, you can always tell when the relationship is turning serious, because he'll give you a diamond. But when you're dating an old man, you know the relationship is serious when he gives you his pillbox. A diamond says forever, but a pillbox says Monday through Sunday—and with an option for refills.

He's always trying to get me to be health conscious. Last night he made me a prune daiquiri. Don't knock 'em; they're good for you. Here's something I've learned: don't serve them with bean dip—ever.

Every once in a while I have to give him one of those pills that make him last longer. You know . . . nitroglycerin. You were thinking Viagra? Viagra pills are blue, heart pills are white. You only make that mistake *once*.

My life is completely different now. Based on my "guests," I've had to learn CPR, I have 9-1-1 on speed dial, and in my night stand I no longer keep a vibrator; I keep a defibrillator. I no longer yell, "Yes! Yes!" It's more like, "Clear! Clear!"

The Pole Dancer

Vikki Claflin

After the success of our date night, recommended in the article "10 Ways to Bring Back the Romance in Your Marriage," I thought I'd pick another suggestion for this week. "Try something sexy and fun that you've never done before," was No. 4. As my mind began a quick visual reel of possibilities, I immediately ruled out naked tandem bungee jumping or partner swapping (unless I get Robert Redford, and my husband takes the homeless woman living under the bridge), and I finally settled on one of the author's ideas. I decided to learn to pole dance.

I know what you're thinking. This probably wasn't the obvious choice. Yes, I'm aware that I'm fifty-seven, I've never done this before, my gene pool leans more toward sturdy German peasant stock than limber Romanian gymnast, and I have Parkinson's. What the hell. Go big or go home, as they say. I promptly ordered a *Pole Dancing for Beginners* DVD and eagerly awaited the lessons on how to wow my man.

Of course, figuring out the pole part of the kit was a bit tougher. When you live in a small town, this isn't something you can just order and have delivered with no questions asked, especially when you dated the UPS guy in high school. When he asks, "What's new with you?" as he delivers your porn pole, he *really* wants to know. Three days later, my DVD arrived, and

I immediately popped it in, ready to get started rocking my husband's world.

Since I didn't have an actual pole, I decided to improvise with the wooden pillar that separates the kitchen from the living room. Silently offering up a prayer that "weight bearing" was meant literally, I grabbed hold with both hands, and prepared to execute my first exotic dance move.

1. The Wrap-Around. Grab the pole. Stick one leg out, swing it to the side, step and pivot (bending the knee to make it more graceful), hook the pole with your outside foot, and finish by arching your back. Uh . . . no. I grabbed the pole with one hand, swung a leg out to the side, whacking my foot on the indoor ficus plant, stepped and pivoted, twisting my ankle as I hooked the pole, then limped on to the Big Finish, energetically arching my back and swinging one arm up overhead, immediately causing a nasty back spasm, accompanied by repeated involuntary yelps of "Owee, owee, owee!" Okay, then. Apparently we need less enthusiasm, more technique.

2. The Basic Climb. This is the stripper version of rope climbing in eighth-grade physical education class, but in less clothes. Since I was unsure whether the thin wooden pillar would withstand my 120-pound attempt to mount it, I decided to improvise and try a door casing.

   Blithely ignoring the tremor in my left arm and the chronic, medication-induced foot spasms, I grabbed hold of the bathroom doorjamb and began my ascent. Note to self: when you need two arms and two legs to do something, and only one of each works with any consistency, consider skipping that exercise. Thirty seconds later, I was a tangled heap on the floor, mortified as I realized that all the blinds were open and the delighted neighbors were gathering in the driveway to watch the show.

3. The Fireman Spin. Ha. I've got this one down. Small leap, grab the pole, bend the knees, and let centrifugal force spin you repeatedly around the pole until you stick the landing with small back arch and a flourish of the arm. Piece of cake. Until I flourished before I stopped spinning. I spun off the pole and into the front door, cracking my head on the doorknob. Yeah, that'll leave a mark.

4. The Body Wave. Basically this is a full-body undulation, while hanging onto the pole with one arm and leaning out. Like most Parkinson's patients, I struggle a little with coordination activities, specifically like my body waving in one direction and my arm going in another. It looked less like an erotic pole dance, and more like I was frantically flagging down an ambulance on a deserted street. Moving on.

5. The Backwards Wiggle. Stand up with your back to the pole, grab said pole with hands up behind your head, then gyrate your hips as you slide down. Seriously? First of all, I'm not built for

gyrating. I couldn't gyrate in college, when I was considerably younger, fifteen pounds thinner, and my appendages only shook when I told them to. All attempts at gyrating simply looked like I'd just been tasered. But I did discover that when I put my hands up behind my head, it inexplicably increased the tremors, resulting in a fairly impressive shimmy. This one could work. It's all about making lemonade, people.

So that evening when my husband came home, I proudly announced my new secret skill. Not surprisingly, he was thrilled and immediately settled in, happily anticipating my Big Move. I decided on the Fireman Spin, letting my body weight do most of the work. I grabbed the pole, swung out my leg to get a good spin going, tucked the other heel up under my butt, and flashed my brightest "Come get me, sailor" smile as I twirled past him.

On the second twirl, my foot cramped up and my arm had a seismic tremor that caused me to let go of the pole and sail across the room, landing on top of a surprised husband with a thud, sending him into unrestrained laughter while he choked out, "That was awesome. Do it again!"

It's been two days and he can't stop laughing. And he still thinks it was supposed to be like that. I'm not telling him otherwise. But I'm thinking of teaching a pole dancing class at the next Parkinson's convention. We've still got the moves.

The Power of the Fishnets

DEBORAH TOMPKINS

I had been out of the dating world for years, and sex wasn't even on my radar screen. I was too busy establishing a new life as a single working mom. At age fifty I divorced, after having been married for twenty-five years.

As time went on, I dated a bit, but found that dating wasn't any easier the second time around. I decided I would only consider fun, interesting men, who wouldn't add stress to my life. However, these men proved to be few and far between.

One day I was invited to attend a fundraising event by a lawyer friend of mine who booked and paid for the band. It was a well-established rock 'n' roll band whose leader was a good friend of my friend.

After the event, I was invited to go for a drink with some friends, including the bandleader. We all piled into one car, and as I climbed in, my dress rose up and exposed my fishnet stockings, which I rarely wore. For some reason, I decided to wear them that night. There is something fun and sexy about fishnet stockings, and the bandleader definitely noticed.

Over a drink, we had a chance to talk. I discovered that he was a fun and interesting guy. He was also divorced after a long-time marriage, and we were about the same age. Best of all, neither of us was looking for a serious relationship, just fun and compatibility.

I started to go to his band gigs, and we began to date. I quickly found out the meaning of "Sex, Drugs, and Rock 'n' Roll." The rock 'n' roll was great, although the drugs were for blood pressure and diabetes. But I was totally surprised by his sex drive at this age.

As time went on, he planned some amazing sexual adventures for us, and he bought me some risqué clothing to wear. He didn't care about the bulges or extra pounds because he had them, too. It helped me feel more confident and less inhibited. So, I became his willing accomplice.

Busy working at my desk one day, he called.

"How tall are you?"

"What are you buying?"

"Never mind."

On our next date, I opened my gift. It was a complete fishnet outfit, including stockings, panties, and a scoop-neck top with garters to hold up the stockings. I had to laugh. Although it took me a while to figure out how to get into it, I felt sexy, and *he was ecstatic.*

We've been together for almost eight years now. He has gotten me other "outfits," but the fishnets remain his favorite. One New Year's Eve, the band had a gig at a casino, and we had rooms for the night. It was a fun gig, and my guy put his heart and soul into his performance. Afterwards, he was exhausted. He was also frustrated because he had wanted us to have a romantic evening, and he didn't have much energy left. When he left the room to get some ice, I put on the fishnets. When he came back, his eyes lit up, and the party started. Happy new year.

All relationships have their ups and downs, and ours is no different. One time we had a serious disagreement, and we didn't see each other for a couple of weeks. I feared the relationship might be over. Then, he had a gig close to my house, so I invited him over to talk when he was done.

During the course of our relationship, he would occasionally stop at the local gas station and buy me a single rose. I knew if he brought me a rose, things would be okay. When he came to my door, he was holding a rose, and I was thrilled. I told him to relax and give me a minute to change. I returned wearing the fishnets, and things were back to normal.

We've gone on several vacations together, and the fishnets always come with us. They have become a symbol of the joy and love we have for each other. Sex keeps us young, and who doesn't want to be desired at any age? Best of all, after the fishnets there is always "skin time." We just lie in each other's arms and relish the moment. This time is so precious because we don't know how many moments we have left.

This winter, we planned a trip to Palm Springs. The only part of the trip that I don't like is packing; I always take too many clothes. The night before we left, we were talking about this on the phone, and right before we hung up, he said, "Don't forget the fishnets!"

Goal Setting Can Be Fun

SUE BROWN

In 1988, I got divorced after living with a man who would remind me whenever he could, "You should be grateful I married you because no one else would even think about it." My self-esteem was shot, and it took years to have the courage to leave the situation and his daily verbal abuse. I was scared of being a single mom with three boys, but I couldn't delay it any longer.

Now, my kids are adults with children of their own, and I am in a happy place in my life. After many years of concentrating on my career, I decided it was time for me to spend time on improving myself. I changed my eating habits, lost a lot of weight, and felt pretty good about myself—in fact, better than I ever had. On the edge of retirement, strange and surprising thoughts began to come into my life: before I die, I want to have hot, torrid sex. Who has a goal like that? Alone in my kitchen, I laughed at the notion. I think I even blushed as I made myself a mug of tea. Was I too old? Would I even know how to have hot, torrid sex, and who would want me? Were any of those things my ex always told me true?

The idea wouldn't leave me. Several of my friends began online dating, were going out on dates and having fun. I was curious, but was scared to try it. One lonely Sunday afternoon,

Your Glasses Are on Top of Your Head

I wanted to look at who was on these dating sites. Little did I know you have to answer all sorts of questions before you can look. I got to the end of the questions and it was do-or-die time. I called a girlfriend and told her what I was doing and why. We laughed, and she guided me through the process of writing a profile about myself. I couldn't believe I was actually following through as she coached me on the phone.

"Just think of it as entertainment. It's not like you are going to marry this person. You are just going to meet for some coffee. No strings attached. This will be fun!"

My thoughts screamed, I want to do it, but I'm too chicken. I am old—who would want to go out with me? If it's just for entertainment, maybe it would be okay. I'll just pretend I am talking to my brother.

I finished my profile, included my photo (cropped from a picture of my grandson and me), wrote down my work email (better safe than sorry—right?), and pushed "send." When I got to work on Monday, I had fifteen emails from the online dating company. I was horrified, and quickly realized it would not be good to have these at work. I forwarded them to my home mail, and changed my email to receive them at home in the future. Soon, even more came, and I was in heavy demand. Who would believe it? One week I met five different guys. Many of them were very different from me, but it was still fun to get to know so many, and with each one I would do my inward screening. Will this be the one I choose for hot, torrid sex?

Confiding in my close friends, I was afraid that my "well" had dried up and may not work anymore.

Horrified, I asked, "Did you know even your private areas get gray hair?"

Fascinated by my naiveté, my girlfriends took me to an adult gift store that night. I was overwhelmed by the sizes, colors, and gadgets designed to find out if the pump needed priming. I was game, made my purchase quickly, and got out of there before I would run into someone I knew. We giggled as we left the store, and I had to promise to give reports later on if I found the gadgets helpful to get back in the game. I was happy to report the juices still flowed and I was pumped and ready for action.

Soon after I met a nice man who I found easy on the eyes and was a good conversationalist, and we had a lot in common. He helped me achieve my goal *over and over.* A couple days later I called my sister and told her I ended up with a bladder infection. Laughing hysterically she said, "What do you expect if you haven't had any action in twenty-five years?"

I discovered just because you are getting older doesn't mean you can't still have sex, and a lot of it. I found out I do enjoy reaching my goals, over and over.

Speed Dating

RENEE RONGEN

I was about to give a presentation for a women's group in upstate New York. Before my talk I like to visit with the women coming in and I noticed three very sharp, nicely dressed elderly women approaching. They were all excited, and told me they just came in from their first experience of speed dating.

Curious, I couldn't help but ask them about it.

"What was it like?"

The first one giggled. "You know, you only get ten minutes to interview them. Those ten minutes go really fast." These women were adorable, and I would guess were in their seventies and eighties. With their sassy attitudes and classy looks, they were younger than their years.

The second one explained more.

"Well, we thought we'd go to that speed dating because none of us is taken right now, and we heard it's all the rage. You go from guy to guy, interviewing them. The only bad thing was that we didn't see anyone our age. One guy was early fifties, and he was lovely to talk to, and I had so much fun."

The third one interjected, "I couldn't help but sound like a grandma when I was with each person. I'd ask, 'Where are you going in your life? Do you have a faith?' I felt there was a good chance he probably wasn't going to ask me out."

They were so proud of themselves for trying it, and so I asked, "Do you think you'll try it again?"

They all giggled and one said, "Maybe if there was an age limit, but we had to try it once."

Oftentimes when I ask people about stepping outside their box, we talk about challenges. These three women were sitting in the front row, and became part of my speech. When I called on them and told the audience they had just come from speed dating, you could see people straining to see who they were. So I had them stand up, turn around, and wave at everyone. The place howled in laughter, and the three of them took bows like rock stars at the end of a fabulous concert.

A year later I returned again to give a presentation for this group, and in the front row three women were waving to me as I began to speak. I squinted against the stage lights and walked closer to the edge of the stage to get a closer look. I started laughing and blurted out, "Are you my sassy speed-dater friends?" The three of them gave me huge smiles as I talked of meeting them the year prior and telling about their adventure. With loads of laughter from the crowd, I asked, "Are you still available, or have you taken yourselves off the dating market?"

The crowd roared, and as clapping subsided, one of the ladies yelled out, "We are online now, on 50-plus match.com," and the place erupted again.

Spooning

Brenda Elsagher

I have never sat next to anyone on a plane who can fall asleep like I do, before the plane has even reached the coasting altitude. I am zonked until they come around with the beverages. Then I usually wake up and drink something. This time I slept right through the ninety-minute flight, and so did the guy next to me. When he sat down next to me, I noticed he had long legs, and we both chatted about how happy we were to get on the flight, we didn't care where we sat.

When I woke up his legs were spooning mine. The plane landed, and he woke up and smiled at me. As I've gotten older, my filter has diminished because I don't worry so much anymore about what people think.

I said, "I believe we slept together."

Without hesitation he said, "It was good for me, was it good for you?"

"I think it was. Just like at home, I can almost sleep through anything."

It was a good laugh, and we chatted until we were at our gate.

Section VII
Health and Happiness

"The more the heart is nourished with happiness,
the more it is insatiable."

—GABRIELLE ROY

The Surprise Runner

KAY CASKEY

I came late to running. I took Running 101 at the local community college in my forties, and have been running ever since. I have always been good at it. It's just one foot in front of the other. I love it. Prior to running, my sports career, which was reigning as jacks queen of my fifth grade, ended in elementary school. I was pre-Title IX. Back then the gym teachers didn't even let us girls run full-court basketball. Apparently they thought our uteruses would drop out.

I have been running ever since, and I am now in my seventies. I have lovely wrinkles on my face, and my abs and gluts are a bit flabby. However, I have great legs. I am lucky to not have varicose veins. My long years of running have shaped my calves in a very muscular way, and from the back, you can't tell how old I really am.

I know this because a couple of years ago, running along a country road, a car full of teenage boys passed me, whistling and hooting loudly—mistakenly thinking, no doubt, that women appreciate and are flattered by being wolf-whistled on the road. Rather than feel threatened and objectified, imagine their surprise when they saw my very mature face, and realized they had just wolf-whistled someone who could have been their grandmother. The horror on their faces remains a delicious memory.

Alligators Are Ackey

Rae Ellen Lee

One day an alligator bit my butt. Almost as strange as that, I was living aboard a sailboat in Seattle with my new husband.

It was a cold, Winnie the Pooh sort of day in March. Bundled in layers of wool and rain gear, I was strolling along the dock, watching a ponytailed geezer about my age deftly motoring his sailboat into the harbor. Not only was he causing a big stir in the no-wake zone, he was wearing only a T-shirt and a skimpy black Speedo, one that barely contained a sizeable bulge.

At exactly that moment, the alligator chomped down hard between my buns, cutting short my state of awe. As Speedo Man disappeared behind a large powerboat, I picked up my pace, traversed two more docks, climbed a steep ramp that connected all the docks to land, and scurried across a parking lot to the nearest toilet. There I discovered my own sizeable bulge, and what turned out to be more than one alligator: it was a case of hemorrhoids.

For days this new plight dominated my attention. I forgot all about Speedo Man. When I took my daily walk into town, the reptiles swung back and forth behind me, intent on taking me down. I was living a predator-prey scene. As I struggled to walk normally, people driving past slowed and stared, as if watching *Wild Kingdom* on TV. Or maybe they thought I was talking to myself. I did catch myself gesturing while schmoozing the creatures, pleading with them to relax back into their warm, dark habitat.

Until I learned otherwise in a biology class, I'd always thought of my rectum by a term that included the word ackey. As a child, if I encountered an electrical outlet, mud, or any sort of feces, my mother would yell, "No! That's ackey!" and I would freeze. Now I wish she'd warned me about other things to watch out for when I grew up, like men who wanted to live on sailboats.

I began to feel that my bulging beasties represented my life—past and present. Twenty-six years ago I'd had surgery for hemorrhoids, after which I went on living, assuming I was immune. Suddenly, here they were, popping out like skeletons that had, until now, stayed where ackey things belonged. Why had they returned? In the classic self-help book *You Can Heal Your Life*, Louise Hay suggests that constipation, the precursor to hemorrhoids, reveals one's difficulty in letting go of the past. Might this include my inability to escape the present?

Or was it because we'd been given a bread machine, and were trying new recipes to the tune of a loaf a day? That's a lot of gluten.

During the time of the occupation of the allied alligators, my husband and I were scheduled to meet a man we didn't know at a coffee shop to discuss teaching English as a second language. My husband entertained this as his next career and, he assumed, it would be mine as well. He shared with me what he told the man on the phone so he'd recognize us. "I'm a tall, silver-haired gentleman. My wife has brown hair, mostly, and a case of hemorrhoids." He wouldn't have actually said that, I felt certain, but when I laughed hysterically, the alpha 'rrhoid grew testy and snapped his teeth.

Later at the library I searched the worldwide web for information on my ailment, and learned new and shiny terms: transit time, bowel tones, sphincter muscles, and fluffy fecal matter. These words used by the medical community replaced other words, in addition to ackey, that had always come to mind so easily; no need to mention them here. On preparationH.com I discovered that 83 percent of all humans will silently suffer this humiliating condition at some time in their lives. Yet no one talks about it with their friends, and certainly not their enemies. Hemorrhoids are not one of the more popular afflictions. But if so many people suffer this debilitating ailment, where were the grants for education and awareness, or to pay for research, maybe even find a cure? Where were the fun runs "for the cure"?

The alligators and I migrated from the library to a drugstore to check out the products available for my problem. We left with a sack of salves and inserts, some surgical gloves to use during the application process, a bottle of stool softener pills, and a canister with 114 teaspoon-doses of 100 percent natural psyllium husk fiber to mix with water and drink during cocktail hour.

To guarantee success, I stopped off at a place selling crystals and smudges and the like. I would take no chances. I even purchased a small voodoo doll, and put a curse on my curse.

Back at the boat, I placed the voodoo doll in a prominent spot, and began my regimen of meds. I also threw the bread machine overboard, stepped up my intake of liquids, and cut my general food consumption by about half, which, nutritionally speaking, was still more food than I needed.

Almost immediately, the alligators disappeared. Perhaps they slithered off in search of their next prey. In any case, I was back on the docks, hoping to spot that guy wearing the bulging Speedo.

An Unusual Thank You

TANYA FUAD

I was born in Baghdad, Iraq, to a Kurdish father and an American mother from Minnesota. In 1991, I worked with Kurdish refugees in Silopi Camp.

In March of 1991, a million or more Kurds had fled to the mountains in fear of Saddam Hussein's advancing army. Many people were falling ill and lining up to be treated by doctors under makeshift plastic tarps. Among them was a man who claimed to be ninety-nine years old. As he waited his turn in line, he smoked a cigarette. The doctor was seeing children and the elderly first. One by one the doctors were distributing medicine for severe cases of dysentery because there was no clean water to drink along the way.

When it was finally the elderly man's turn, the doctor said, "I see you are not too sick to smoke. How many years have you smoked?"

"Sir, I am ninety-nine, so I believe I have smoked for perhaps ninety years."

"So you aren't feeling good? How can I help you?"

The man said, "I'm constipated."

The doctor raised his hands to the sky and thanked Allah, and told the man, "Sir, I have spent the last five days treating dysentery. I am happy to finally treat this problem. My advice to you is to keep doing whatever it is you are doing, and remember to thank God for every day."

New Experiences in the USA

BAHGAT ELSAGHER

When my father traveled from Egypt to the USA for a visit, he did not speak any English. We noticed he couldn't walk very well and blamed it on the long flight, but over time we discovered he had multiple health issues. I took him to his first physical exam ever. People in Egypt, as well as many other cultures, do not go to the doctors unless they absolutely have to because "preventative care" is not part of their understanding.

Upon explaining to my dad what is going to happen at the clinic, I intentionally didn't tell him about the prostate exam as part of the physical exam procedure. I stepped out to give him some privacy while he was taking down his pants. As I was exiting the room, I could see the panic in his eyes, as if he was asking me not to leave him alone in the room with this doctor.

Shortly afterward on the other side of the door, I could hear my dad shouting at the doctor in Arabic and swearing frantically. When he left the room after getting his clothes back on he said, "At this age and after all these years, I finally come to the United States of America to experience a doctor who wants to check my personal parts! I feel like I just lost my virginity at seventy-three years of age!"

A couple days later I was going to take my father to another doctor's appointment to get his eyes checked because he had major cataracts. I told him to go sit in the car and wait for me, and I'd be there in a minute.

When I got to the car, he wasn't there. I found him sitting in a stranger's car having a cigarette. He had been a smoker in Egypt but we explained the health problems with smoking, and he stopped smoking while he lived with us. The cigarettes were just sitting in the car, so he helped himself while he waited for us. He was getting more confused too, but he made himself comfortable, and apparently the guys who were roofing the house next door were getting a kick out of the scene unfolding below.

"Dad, this is not my car. No, you can't take the cigarettes with you. Where did you find this cooler? Were you eating the guy's food? We need to leave it here, Dad, come with me now."

One of the main health issues my dad had when he came to visit was a knee problem, which turned out to be a symptom of undiagnosed Parkinson's disease. We coped the best we could, and kept having fun with him, allowing more time for getting places. So many things were new for him, things we had taken for granted he would know. He was still struggling with the culture shock, and did not know the basics of how to flush the toilet, and I often went into the bathroom after him to make sure the toilet was flushed.

After a weekend along the north shore of Lake Superior, we stopped at a casino buffet on the way home. After dinner, and before we got back on the road, my father was interested in finding the bathroom. I showed him where it was, and found a long line in front of the men's restroom. He waited patiently for his turn, and after he used the bathroom, I tried to rush in right behind him to flush the toilet for the next person. Instead, the next person in line obstructed me and did not allow me to go in, perhaps thinking I was taking his turn. I reluctantly let the guy go in, and I could hear him swearing.

"God almighty, mother of God, you must not have s—t for a month! This is the biggest dump I have ever seen." I was laughing my guts out, feeling sorry for the guy, and in the meantime, my dad had no clue what had just happened or what the guy said. We both walked out smiling, feeling much better.

The Lessons in Caregiving

Mary Drago

Throughout my thirties, forties, and fifties, I learned I had to keep a sense of humor about what life has thrown not only at me, but also at my loved ones. Having been a caregiver now for many years, I think about the two women who have taught me that pain, hope, and humor go hand in hand.

I have been a caretaker since age fifteen when my dad had his first stroke. Then my mother was diagnosed with stage 3C breast cancer when she was sixty-six and I was thirty-three. My mother-in-law was diagnosed with Alzheimer's disease when I was in my forties, and came to live with us for almost fifteen years.

My mother was always positive, even though I'm sure she was filled with anguish at having a radical mastectomy with removal of thirty lymph nodes, all of which were positive.

When her cat used to lie on her chest, she would say, "She knows to lie on the side that is flat and comfortable."

When she had to undergo a grueling year of chemo after surgery, the first question she asked her oncologist was, "When can I go to Atlantic City?" She *loved* the slots.

Her physician laughed and said, "Andria, this is what is going to get you through this!" The day after she finished chemo, she was on a bus with me to go to Atlantic City. When she turned seventy, away we went, and took one of those push-cart rides on the Boardwalk, and we laughed so much. What a treasured memory.

Her final wish was to die in the house my dad had bought fifty years before. So I put her on home hospice, and moved back home to care for her with my husband's blessing.

"You do what you have to do. I'll be here to catch you if you fall." At the same time I was caring for Mom, my husband had his mother with advanced Alzheimer's in our house.

My mother-in-law, Betty, was a whole different animal. I was the "nice lady" who cared for her, and my husband was the "nice man." She would sit on the porch, have a cup of tea, and just smell the spring air as I sat with her. She taught me patience, to be gentler, to slow down—and to savor the now. I slowed my steps, my speech, even my impatience toward her. She recognized it in some part of her soul because she would thank me, and give me the sweetest smile.

Betty worked in the "code breaking" area of the military during WWII. To see her reduced to this state was truly heartbreaking. But I have to say, both she and my mom took joy in simple pleasures, pizza and a DVD, a good cup of coffee, a hearty laugh, and joy in nature. Mom used to say, when she was confined to just the living room, "Open the blinds so I can see the beautiful sky."

I know there is pain and always will be. But I have learned to take joy in the small things for they are what matters, and keep laughing. Mom often quoted a saying in Greek: "Those who have hope will never be lost." Knowing she was near the end, she'd say to my husband and me, "Just love each other."

I think more globally these days, and this simple message might be all we need to do—just love each other.

We Have Liftoff: Getting a Colonoscopy

Dan Van Oss

About age fifty, your colon, if you don't have it checked out, has been known to reach up through your body and strangle you in the night. Well, not really, but this is the type of urgency the Colon Cancer Alliance would like to convey to you about getting a colonoscopy after fifty. You may, like many people, assume having a colonoscopy realistically portrayed like a terrified, sci-fi movie farmer being probed by tentacled aliens in their cold, antiseptic spaceship. This is a common misconception, as modern colonoscopy science has long since done away with tentacles, although the probes are still pretty cold.

I have found there are several phases.

Phase One: Fueling for Launch

Most people complain the worst part of a colonoscopy procedure is the preparation, much like the worst part of preparing for a test is how much the CliffsNotes cost. One of these products, if the FDA had been doing its job correctly, should have been named "GoConstantly." Drinking this product will be the closest you ever get to heaven, if heaven were a place where all you had to drink was thick and sticky bobcat sputum.

Scientists are constantly expanding the field of poop-induce-ment products, so take heart. Maybe by the time you read this, they will have invented a removable colon you can pull out like a vacuum cleaner hose.

Phase Two: Liftoff

You and your toilet will now be on first-name terms, as it will soon become your closest friend. I called mine Tex. I had many conversations with Tex, various discussions about the basics of rocket propulsion, how nature abhors a vacuum, Old Faithful—you know, the usual. I suspect, however, by the end of the day he was tiring of my conversation, and I had devel-oped a strange, superhuman craving for a taco.

Phase Three: Orbit

You will awake early the next morning feeling for some reason like an empty sausage skin, and with an overpower-ing desire to eat the couch cushions. As your significant other drives you to the hospital, he or she will be sure to pass every doughnut shop and fast-food place on the way, with their deli-cious scents of American fat wafting in the air, just to remind you—*you haven't eaten in a day.* Once at the hospital, you will exchange your street clothes for a loose paper tablecloth with a suspicious opening in the back, and some rubber-treaded tan hospital socks that are not interested in staying up your ankles. Now it's needle time.

I like getting my blood drawn just about as much as I like having a sharp metal tube plunged into my flesh to suck out my vital bodily juices—oh, wait, it's the same thing. So I warned the nurses that if I started turning white, it was only because they were poking a hollow steel rod into my hand. Normally, sharp objects are something a mom yells at you to avoid, yet here was my wife encouraging them. The nurses seemed to understand, as their smirks implied they had dealt with men before. So, once my unmanliness card, as well as my hand, was punched, we were ready to roll to the procedure room.

Phase Four: Rear Entry

Your doctor, who will seem to be grinning a little too much for some reason, is waiting for you with a flexible tube called a colonoscope, which sounds like a bad fifties' movie gimmick ("See *Spartacus*, now in Colonscope!"). Knowing where this tube will be used, we did ask how many times it had been, uh, "used" before, and we were assured there was a technician whose specific job it was to boil it in acid in an active volcano after every use.

At this point, you may be slightly nervous, but don't worry, your doctor and nurses have done these thousands of times without once making a joke about full moons. They are all professionals, and as such are very appreciative you made them get up at 6 a.m. so they could look at your butt. Once the doctor says count backwards from ninety-nine, you're home free, as the room will now appear to shrink into the distance, and you begin a wonderful dream about eating a "full breakfast" soon. This is the easy part, as all you're required to do is be unconscious; it's the doctor and nurses who have to live with their actions the rest of their lives.

Expect to wake up feeling refreshed and somehow slightly violated, but most likely with a clean bill of health, as I was, and ready for the biggest breakfast your colon has ever seen. Now if I can only stop dreaming about vacuum cleaners.

The Golf Handicap

BRENDA ELSAGHER

One of my clients told me a story about her brother. He and his wife had become snowbirds in Arizona to get away from the cold Minnesota weather. Since they would be living there for a few months every year, they decided to take up the sport of golf.

They were on their way to their first golf lesson when the husband asked the wife if she had filled out the paperwork. "Of course!" she replied. Glancing at the registration paper he was about to hand over to the golf pro, he noticed the line: "Fill in your handicap here _____." She had written in "Parkinson's."

Hard of Hearing

EDNA L. THAYER

My husband was very hard of hearing. As we were driving along the highway one day, I saw two deer in the ditch. We had hit a deer with our car before, and neither the deer nor the car came out good, so I did not want it to happen again.

I hollered, "There's some deer in the ditch."

My husband responded, "Mine do, too!"

"What do you think I said?"

"Didn't you say your ears itch?"

All who knew my husband, including family, knew he was hard of hearing. When he died at age eighty-two, a great-grand-daughter had just turned three at the time of his celebration of life. When the casket in front of the church was closed at the beginning of the service, she became very upset and said, "Tell them to open the lid back up so Grandpa can hear!"

New Year's Revolt-lutions

LAURIE FABRIZIO

It was 12:01 a.m. on New Year's Day. Dick Clark's computer-generated avatar just announced the ball had dropped in Times Square. Anorexic dancers with barely there outfits so tight they appeared to have been airbrushed on gyrated across the TV screen. The performer grabbed his crotch for the fiftieth time while shouting his latest hit to screaming teenagers. One couldn't help but wonder if he was suffering from a bad case of crabs, or if he had tumble-dried his jockey shorts on high.

Commercial break . . .

"Are you tired of those unwanted pounds you packed on during the holidays? Is your underwear producing wedgies, and your jeans giving you the adorable muffin-top look?"

I switched the channel.

Thin, perky promoters from every diet group known to man (and woman) spewed their sales pitches with annoyingly catchy tunes. I hadn't even swallowed my last Christmas cookie when they swarmed like senior citizens at an early bird special.

"I didn't like what I saw in the mirror so I decided I needed to lose fifty pounds. Ta-da!" The singer gushed as she proudly modeled her chiseled size-two figure.

Amazing what liposuction, a boob job, and plastic surgery will do for you.

I wanted to shout, "Hey, what do you do if you have a chest of a thirteen-year-old boy, have luscious love handles, and sport your own back-up camera?"

Maybe I didn't want to lose weight. What were they all insinuating? Perhaps I liked my double chin. Who said my maternity clothes from 1987 were outdated? I always preferred round-to-hourglass figures anyways. I considered myself "Ruben-esque." By any reasonable definition, I was in shape.

I could walk to the refrigerator without getting winded, could hoist myself off the couch without a crane, and drive to the mailbox on really cold days without stopping to pee. They said to eat leafy greens, so all-you-can-eat salad bar, here I come. I had a squashed protein bar in my purse; who said I don't have good intentions? Besides, I didn't want to look like a stick person. My idol was one who yo-yo diets through life.

Then my privacy was hacked. Weight loss ads, exercise promos, and magic fat reducers invaded my email. I received text alerts. Solicitors plagued me with annoying dinnertime phone calls. They were stalking me. Flipping through my favorite channels, I saw emaciated Barbie clones were everywhere. A fuchsia-adorned actress and weight-loss spokeswoman sneered at me with her ruby plumped lips.

"I lost fifty pounds. Even 'you' can do it!"

Amazing what a full-body elastic suit will do.

What would I be met with next . . . the scale police? Didn't I throw it out with my thigh master? Disgusted, I invented a solution. I would hook my navel up to my laptop with a USB cable, thus allowing my excess fat to be uploaded straight to the cloud. It would then be donated to anorexic models and actresses in need. They want me to lose the weight in six weeks, great. I'll send it to them in an email. Better yet, a text message, or a tweet.

My driver's license now has the "fat donor box" checked. So back off.

In the meantime, here are my other New Year's revolt-lutions:

- I will no longer use my treadmill as a drying rack. The dogs need exercise; it worked for Astro from *The Jetsons.*

- I will remove the dumbbells from under my bed, after I blow off the dusty patina.

- I will stop eating sweets, unless they are chocolate-based, which is good for your heart, and helps with menopause.

- I will be more innovative about my excuses not to exercise.

- I will cook healthy meals for my family, which must include potatoes, pasta, or bread.

- I will stop consuming alcoholic beverages as soon as I finish this bottle of wine.

- I will encourage family and friends to join me in my healthy endeavor, as soon as they stop laughing. Okay—I tried this last year.

- I will stop flipping off thin, fit people. I do suffer from Tourette's of the finger.

- I will always wear black. The fashion police deem it a classic, and my mirror claims it is thinning.

Why is aging so vilified? It's a natural progression for all of us. Why can't we accept who we are, what we are, and how we look . . . and just be happy with it? This insatiable desire to look forever young is nothing but a lust for skin-deep beauty. We are obsessed with what we look like on the outside, when we would be better off worrying about what is on the inside. So, have an occasional chocolate chip cookie, and follow it with an eight-ounce water chaser. After all, life is full of compromises.

Facing Surgery with Humor
Linda MacNeal

A few years back, the warranty on some of my body parts must have expired without the courtesy of a renewal request. Lots of my frequent flyer parts were grounded, and so was I. Since I'm old—oops, excuse me, I mean, aged to perfection—it was somewhat inevitable, I suppose.

First off, I bemoaned my fate and barfed negativity about my uncooperative body parts. But this story is not about my inevitable grounding, it's about how I triumphed. I believe I did an exemplary job of aging joyfully during a series of three orthoscopic joint surgeries.

So how could this happen to a "nice girl like me" who exercises, eats the Surgeon General's recommended diet, and votes the right way? My excuse is that I was a college gymnast in the 1960s. The uneven bars were much closer together in the old days, and we performed on cement floors with little or no floor matting, and later, I ran five New York City marathons.

One of the popular uneven parallel bar moves was called a "dislocate"-type catch. Its name explains exactly what it did to our shoulders. Sometimes we were fortunate, and were able to use the wrestling team's mats for our dismounts, which was no bargain either because it made it harder to stick a landing. Most gymnasts of the 1960s are probably now landing in operating rooms around the country getting overhauls for the damage we did to ourselves in the then-new sport of gymnastics.

Is there ever a convenient time for surgery? This was a particularly inconvenient time for my parts to walk off the job. Isn't there a Patient Bill of Rights that everyone is entitled to a few months to limp around and be waited on? Even under ideal circumstances, I can't imagine being waited on, but let's stick to the facts—reality is entertaining enough. For example, my husband was drafted into the army during the Vietnam War, and thirty-four years later was now awaiting a deployment to Iraq as an army reserve officer. So we were in a hurry to get the surgeries completed quickly, and scheduled them at two-week intervals.

My life's purpose is to live as an example of personal peace and self-generated humor. I live and teach these principles in all I do. I believe anyone can have fun no matter what the circumstances. It's up to each of us to arrive wherever we go with the right attitude, and make sure people around us are nourished and enjoy themselves.

To set the example in each of my procedures, I wore a sponge clown nose, and wrote funny messages on my body to surprise and entertain the medical professionals, giving everyone who wants to participate a bit of fun. The prep nurse came in to run the IV line with the good legal drugs. She saw my preparations, laughed, and said, "The nurses will really enjoy this!"

For the first surgery, I wrote all over the leg *not* being operated on, explaining this was my good knee, and to leave it alone. On the other leg, I wrote along my shin bone, "This is my bum knee." Then I drew an arrow pointing to the right knee.

Since the staff gave me such a nice reception for this, two weeks later I arrived with writing on both legs. Along the leg whose knee was just operated on I wrote: "This is supposed to be my good knee, if it doesn't look good, you have only yourself to blame." On the leg to be worked on, I wrote a greeting to the surgical staff and also labeled it, "This is the bum knee."

My third visit two weeks later was for shoulder surgery. Just for fun, I went online and used the free template to create a Dummies fake book cover, and named it *Surgery for Dummies*. The book included helpful hints like, "Measure twice, cut once." I attached the book to my shoulder under my elegant hospital gown.

Since I had a bone spur in my shoulder, I made a big green toe-tag saying, "In case things don't go well, list my cause of death as, 'chip on her shoulder.'" I also wrapped yellow *caution* tape around my body.

Later I was told my doctor had expected some sort of prank, but was still pleasantly surprised. He really loved the whole routine. I saw the same doctor years later, and he still remembered me, and said I remain the record holder for the funniest surprise in the operating room when he found the Dummies book.

Why would I bother doing these things? Isn't it easier to simply grin and bear it? I often take the trouble to create fun and memorable moments for people. I've learned it gives me a feeling of control over my fear, and gives everyone else, including me, a good laugh. Laughter is my therapy and keeps all of us relaxed and present.

Those surgeries were the beginning of my life in body graffiti. I showed up for my colonoscopy with happy faces drawn on my butt cheeks. *I had to do it.* So when my by-the-book soldier of a husband wouldn't draw the smiley faces in the requested places, I went to my girlfriend. She drew them on, and of course they were a big hit. My doctor said he had heard of this stunt before, but it was the first time he was privileged to get one from his patient. I am *so very proud.*

Laughing to the End

ALICE MURPHY

My dry-humor brother, John, had numerous heart attacks, but refused to give in to them. Finally "the big one" was getting him. As he was in the hospital with no hope of winning this one, he was of course surrounded by many family members. He complained his back was really hurting. My niece stepped into the hallway and called to the nurses, "Can you give him something? His back is killing him"

John—still the witty one, responded with, "Oh, so it is my *back* that is killing me." About ten minutes later, it did . . .

For some people this might seem awful, but it made us feel better that he could joke all the way to the end of his life. We miss him, but it's a cool story to remember.

Twitchy Gut

Jean di Carlo-Wagner

I've always had a twitchy gut. When I was young, I also had a steel-trap sphincter. However, being a colorectal survivor, I've learned many skills to deal with unpredictable bowels and fast trips to the bathroom. Evacuations, I call them. Everything in my colon is immediately evacuated within seconds. Mostly, I'm very successful at going out, because I can tell you where every toilet is within a fifteen-mile radius of my home.

My husband recently retired, and we somehow acquired two rescue puppies. It was a moment of sheer insanity when we took both of the puppies in the same kennel. Life was starting to become a routine, which was more around their bowel habits than mine. We all agreed to do our business in a timely and dignified manner. It was time to take the six-months-olds on a road trip from San Diego to Denver.

We found, just like kids, the puppies slept while we drove from roadside travelers' relief to roadside travelers' stations. Did you know most of them are *not* dog friendly, which was difficult for the puppies, but really, I'm the most important person in this story, and I could stop and use the facilities. No problem. I was starting to eat road food. We stopped at every single fast-food restaurant along the way for our meals. My gut started to get clogged.

We made it to our destination vacation with loving family awaiting our arrival. The few days of normal food were somewhat helpful. Things were now reacting fairly normally. Normal becomes essential. Heck, all those TV ads about fiber used to annoy me. Now, I listen. In a few days, we said our goodbyes and again hit the road. We took the long way home, and drove through part of the United States barely inhabited by human beings. When we stopped at a dog-friendly hotel, I got a thick, sick feeling of being overdue. Like a late-term pregnancy, things were bearing down on me, and riding for hours at a time was a risky move.

After we rested for the night, I thought I'd blast out the colon clog. I decided to drink alternating apple juice and regular coffee. It's my own personal rescue relief. Usually, it would blast the clog right out of my gut in no time, but it didn't happen. I supposed I was clogged for another two hours. We had to get going so off we drove.

Twenty minutes into the first leg of the trip, twitch. I turned to my husband with not much urgency, and said, "If we come along a roadside station, I think I'm going to need to stop."

His eyebrows narrowed; he had heard this before. "How fast do you need me to stop?"

I started to sweat little beads around my forehead. "Anytime soon would be great."

Another twenty minutes passed without us seeing signs of any kind.

I became desperate. "Just stop at the next gas station. Stop anywhere. I have to go."

He accelerated and focused his full attention on road signs. Like a mad pair of homing pigeons, we turned our heads from side to side. Nothing. Nada.

Sweating fully into my armpits and holding my stomach, in absolute surrender I screamed, "Pull over, I don't care. I've got to go now." Then it appeared. A sign glowing of hope, a bathroom, and maybe some apple pie and leather clothing.

"Take that damn exit!" another woman with my voice squealed. My frightened husband dutifully careened off the exit. "It's gotta be here somewhere." We were driving on an access road running parallel to the freeway. We saw boarded-up houses, dust devils kissing the road, and finally, another sign to my salvation.

We arrived in a parking lot, overgrown with prickly weeds and yes, the store was boarded up, too. In fact, it was a little like driving off the end of the world into a town that screamed Twilight Zone. I feverishly looked at all the tiny boarded-up houses in the area. No one seemed to be around. The saving grace was one old tree, which looked about as out of place as we did. I told my husband to look away; I was going toward the tree. With only one purpose in mind, and shedding all sense of propriety and dignity, I pulled down my pants and let molten lava go.

Out of nowhere, a woman across the street came out into her yard. She looked at me with disgust and disdain. My husband was watching the area from the car, and saw her just as I did. He decided to defend my honor by letting the dogs out of the car. He thought they would hide me. Of course they joined under the tree, sniffing, licking, jumping, and barking. The woman returned to her door and slammed it.

I didn't need a tissue anymore, so I slinked into the car. "Go, go, go!"

The dogs did not want to jump back in the car. My husband got out and gathered them up, and we burned rubber out of the ghost town. We wanted to leave the scene of the crime.

We laughed, and have had a good time telling this story. Love, you see, is about the journey and stages of life, even more so than just reacting to a twitchy gut.

Welcome to Medicare

Anne Bodman

The handy little booklet from the government cheerfully calls it Welcome to Medicare. It's the physical exam they pay for when you become eligible at sixty-five years old. At my appointment with Dr. K, I was poked, prodded, squeezed, and scoped in every orifice. I had an EKG, blood work, eye test, bone scan, mammogram, and Pap smear.

Dr. K read questions off a checklist: "How long does it take you to get rolling in the morning? Is your house free of dangers like slippery little rugs? Do you use street drugs? Do you have more than one sexual partner?"

When I asked about a twinge in my hip, she advised, "We don't worry about twinges; it has to be chronic. And where you're holding—it's not your hip. It looks like the rim of your pelvis. Lots of nerves there."

I tried to make a joke. "Where's my Welcome to Medicare banner, flowers, and cookies? When I bought my new Ford pickup, I got long-stemmed chocolate chip cookies."

"Sorry," Dr. K consoled me, "the welcoming band couldn't make it either."

I left the office feeling decidedly underwhelmed. So this is the threshold of old age.

The next time I particularly noticed my age was Halloween,

when I chose to dress as one of those sex-starved older women they call "cougars." After tugging on very snug pantyhose to "sculpt" my rippling thighs, the black velvet pants and the leopard-print silky top went on just fine—and, yes, I had them in my closet from younger days—but the eyeliner and lipstick were problems. I hadn't worn either for decades.

I took off my glasses and squinted at myself in the mirror. It was hard to see. I had learned as a teenager to stretch my skin at the corner of the eye in order to give a firm surface to apply the eyeliner. I did that, but when I released the skin, the elegant long line I thought I had painted all puckered up into little polka dots. My lid sagged. When I opened my eyes wide, some of the paint transferred to the area under my eyebrow. I was pock marked, with brown-black smears.

Luckily, it all washed off more easily than I had remembered, and I tried again. This time I didn't stretch anything; I just slathered. Then I fanned myself with a newspaper to the count of one hundred before approaching the other eye. And the lipstick? I noticed my mouth didn't seem to be outlined the way it used to be. I had to guess at my lip line. I rolled on the lipstick, sniffing in the nostalgic lipstick smell, and pressed my lips together. There were so many wrinkles there, but from a distance, without my glasses, I looked like a cougar for sure.

The final hint of indignity came when I was trying to paste on the long black fingernails. I needed two helpers to peel and apply my talons. And then, of course, like a kid in a snowsuit, I needed to go to the bathroom, and I lost all my nails unrolling my pantyhose.

The Life-Changing Bike Trip

Brenda Elsagher

For most of my adult life, I weighed over three hundred pounds, and thought I was destined to remain that way. After trying the usual weight-loss methods, I decided to give up, love myself the best I could, and try not to let my weight stop me from doing anything. I still wholeheartedly believe: go for the gusto, and don't wait till everything is perfect in your life or you won't do a thing. I would have missed out on so much if I had waited until my house was clean, my body was slim, or my college degree was finished.

My latest endeavor had to do with attempting to ride a two-wheeled recumbent bike up the mountains and hills of the Seattle area. I had been at a United Ostomy Association of America conference, and heard a man in his fifties who had similar physical challenges in terms of having an ostomy describe his experience doing a three-day, 210-mile ride out of New York in such a way I believed I could do it too. I found this notion heating up inside me from my toes to the top of my head, and couldn't let it go. Perhaps I was delusional, or suffering from indigestion.

After this man's speech, I found the ride director and asked him, "Could a fifty-year-old woman my size, with two bad knees, who hasn't trained for any kind of exercise for the last ten years, do this ride?"

"With proper training and your doctor's okay, I don't see why not."

Shoot, I hadn't expected his response. I thought this crazy idea would disappear at the obstacles I had placed before him. Instead, I formulated a plan to go forward, but make it tougher to actually go.

I didn't have a bike. I didn't want to buy a bike since I'd probably never use it again after this bike trip. One of my clients at the time had told me about how she and her husband ride three-wheeled recumbent bikes, and suggested I check it out. I'd had major surgery, and some of my woman parts were rearranged, and let me be plain here—a regular bike would not work. I needed a big, thick, cushy seat, and recumbents had what I needed.

I also needed to meet the pledge requirement to be able to be a participant, and I needed to ship the bike I didn't have to Seattle and pay for plane fare from Minnesota. This was turning into a much bigger deal than just going on a bike ride. Now I would need money, training, and a bike.

Ever the optimist, I devised a plan I was sure would not work since I secretly had no confidence that I could ride the bike I didn't have, or do the training with the little time I didn't have either. I decided to have a comedy show fundraiser and advertise the bike shop for giving me a bike to use. They would probably never agree to it, so I thought this whole notion would go away. In the meantime, I went to the doctor and had a frank talk about my knees, and if they could endure this trip.

He said, "They are already shot. You need to get them replaced, so it couldn't hurt you any worse than they are right now."

Geez, even he didn't say no.

"I can offer you cortisone shots in your knees, and keep taking the eight hundred milligrams of ibuprofen as needed."

Geez, this might actually happen.

Off to the bike store I went, and introduced myself to the owner. I began to tell him about the Get Your Guts in Gear (GYGIG) bike ride in Seattle, and what the ride was all about.

"Have you ever heard about Crohn's disease or ulcerative colitis?"

He nodded in the affirmative.

"Have you ever heard of people with ostomies? Colostomy? Ileostomy? Urostomies?"

He replied, "You lost-a-me!"

I instantly appreciated his humor, and went into my short speech about people needing surgery because their bowels or bladders have become diseased for one reason or another, and parts or all have been removed, and since we all have to poop or pee or we die, some of us have ostomies.

"We wear a pouch on the outside of our bodies to collect it, which saves our lives. I have one because I had colorectal cancer when I was thirty-nine. I had a golf ball–sized tumor in my rectum, and had to have my rectum removed to save my life. Many people, when they have these surgeries, can never imagine going on a bike ride again, and especially riding all those miles, camping at night in a tent, and doing it for three days. It's an amazing goal to strive for, and they often feel liberated."

"So what can I do for you?" he asked.

I didn't hesitate, or I might have lost my nerve.

"Well, I need a bike, but I don't want to buy one. I doubt I'll keep it up after the training for the bike ride. Is it possible I could borrow one? My friend told me about your three-wheeled recumbent bikes, and she thought it might be good for me since my surgery rearranged my woman parts, and those regular bike seats just don't cut it anymore. I used to enjoy biking but after my surgery, things were never the same again."

Quickly I assessed he wasn't the kind of guy who needed more details. Even though I secretly was afraid to do this bike ride, I couldn't help myself from pushing forward. I told him I was a comic and national speaker, had written a couple of books, and would advertise his store, put the bike up on the stage, and tell the audience about my plan on riding that bike.

Smirking, he said, "So you just want me to lend you a bike for several months while you train for this bike ride held in Washington, and in exchange you'll advertise it at your comedy show?"

"Yes, that's pretty much it," I said, knowing he would never go for this deal.

"Nope, it would never work," he quickly answered. "A trike recumbent bike will not be fast enough. You'll need a two-wheeled recumbent bike. Have you ever ridden one?"

"Ah, nope," was all I could say.

"Let's go outside and I'll show you how it goes."

Oh. My. God. He is as crazy as me.

It was April 1st (of course), with snow banks still on the ground. He showed me the basics on the bike, explained the gears to me, talked about how the balance was different, and gave me a running push-off. I peddled about ten feet before I fell over. Once again, he got next to me, explained a couple more details, and pushed me off again. This time I went partially around the parking lot in the strip mall before I fell over. My husband was with me, and decided to try it too. I secretly felt better when he fell over almost instantly.

"You need a different bike, hold on," the bike store owner said as he dashed back into the store. He returned with a smaller version, and once he pushed me off again, I noticed the people in the other stores had gathered at the front windows watching this spectacle, probably laying down bets how long it would take me to fall down again. I was scared, but made another attempt. This time I got all around the parking lot before I crashed into a snow bank. He sent me home with the bike. I think he just wanted me out of there. We agreed to keep in touch. I would practice on this one until I had logged some miles, and then I would come back for the bigger bike.

Oh. My. God. I am walking out of the bike store with a loaner.

The next morning, I took the bike out for my first ride. I thought I'd attempt to go a mile. My spirits were up even though I was frightened I would fall again. My legs were already bruised.

At the end of the block I successfully maneuvered a turn, and as I approached a very slight incline, I mistakenly shifted the gears the wrong way and keeled over. My pride was hurt more than anything else. It's very hard to push off on a recumbent bike going uphill, so I walked it to level ground. I hopped on it expecting to go, but I could not get my foot to leave the ground. The self-talk began.

Come on, Brenda, you can do this. Just let go. Lift your foot. Push off. Go. Come on girl, you can do this. Go, go, go. For twenty minutes I fought my self-doubts, my insecurities, and my crazy notion that I could actually do this. I was about to start in on the self-deprecating commentary next when a little boy yelled to me from his door.

"Hey, lady, what you doing?"

"I'm riding my bike!"

"No you're not."

His remark made me laugh, and within seconds I was able to lift off, and I rode the bike the block home and left it in the garage for three days before I had the courage to try it again.

That evening I was spending time with my mother who was

dealing with dementia. A previously opinionated woman, she had become soft-hearted and shared her emotions easily.

"Mom, you've got to see something." I rolled up my pants and showed her my bruised legs. "Did you know you could have so many colors of bruises?"

"How did that happen?"

"I am training for a two hundred and ten-mile, three-day bike trip in the state of Washington, and have a new bike I am learning on."

When I looked up at her, she was crying. "Mom, what's wrong?"

She sniffled, "I can't believe you're so stupid!"

I laughed quietly; I saw a glimpse of the feisty mom I used to know. Later in the week, I took my mom along to a talk I was giving at a local church. During my talk I was describing the bike ride I was going to attempt. Some women came up to us afterward, and asked my mom what she thought of her daughter doing this ride.

With her filter gone, she simply said, "She's an idiot!"

Everyone laughed politely, but some of my own thoughts matched hers.

Months later, I returned for the bigger bike, my comedy show went off well, and I raised enough money to get my bike and me to the ride, along with the required pledges. I was on my way. My knees were hanging in there, and most weeks I was training about a hundred miles, knowing I would be expected to ride seventy miles a day. The hills were challenging in Minnesota, and I was doing the best I could.

When I got to Washington and experienced my first "hill," I knew I was in trouble. I cried at the first rest area. I was already being picked up by the sweep van at the bottom of the big hills so I could keep up with the rest of the bikers. I was humiliated by my own fatal optimism.

Sometimes I ended up getting off my bike and pushing it up the hills, but this gave me time to take in the glorious view. I still biked 150 miles in those three days, and I was elated when the ride was over.

Little did I know that the biking would spark the beginning of a personal transformation. I watched the other lean bikers zoom by me, and realized being this large was seriously slowing me down. I let this new realization begin to soak in to my consciousness. I brought my bike back to the store and said, "I'd like to thank you for letting me use this bike, and now I'd like to buy it."

"It's a used bike now; I'd have to sell it to you for cost."

I could have kissed him.

Since my first ride, I've lost half my body size due to quitting sugar, white flour, and giving up drinking adult beverages. Since then, I've gone on two more two-day, 150-mile rides, and was able to complete every mile.

Ironically, having a life-saving ostomy also helped me begin the journey of getting healthier, which also helped me change my mindset of no longer accepting that I am destined to be big. The daily habits I practice have been keeping my weight stable for years, and I am grateful to friends who help me with it one day at a time.

Recently I had a new idea: I think I'll run a 5K. I'm running in parking lots these days; we'll see how much farther I get. Life is an adventure, and just because I am growing older, it doesn't mean I can't challenge myself.

All I need from time to time is to feel content and have a good laugh. A sign hangs in my office with a quote from an anonymous writer, helping me put life in perspective: "Blessed are they who can laugh at themselves, for they shall never cease to be amused."

Contributor Biographies

Ruth Bachman is a cancer survivor, mountain climber, author, and inspiring presenter. Ruth contributes her time, resources, and talents on behalf of cancer research, education, and advocacy, bringing a timeless message to diverse audiences about the one constant in life: change. Ruth's award-winning book is *Growing Through the Narrow Spots*. www.RuthBachman.com, p. 44

Cindy Barefield is a nurse married to a nurse for thirty years. They live happily in a small town outside of Houston, Texas, and are the proud parents of two children and one grandson. As a Wound, Ostomy, Continent (WOC) nurse for ten years, Cindy is proud to share this story of her family as part of Brenda's book. p. 113

Barb Best is a comedy writer whose popular humor blog appears at BarbBest.com and at Humor.Alltop.com. She is the author of *Find Your Funny: The LOL Survival Guide for Teens* with Dr. Joanne Jackal, and *How to Be Miserable: The Missing Manual* (a spoof on *The Happiness Project*). p. 95

Bev Biller has been a WOC nurse for seventeen years, lives in Massachusetts, and enjoys traveling, hiking, camping, and quilting. p. 58

Anne Bodman lives just outside Sturgis, South Dakota, with her husband, Andy, and four-legged friends Zamboni, Flipper, and Jack. A member of the Black Hills Storytellers since 1989, she spins tales "from the sublime to the ridiculous." p. 216

Noreen Braman lives on the Smile Side of Life in Jamesburg, New Jersey. She has numerous published poems, stories, and nonfiction in print and online, and is the author of five books. Information on her writing and Laughter Wellness work can be found at noreensdigitaldreams.com. p. 33

Sue Brown is funny, adventurous, and loves goal-setting not associated with a job. She took a risk and found out late in life that Auntie Mame was right: Live! Live! Live! p. 180

Kay Caskey, MSW, is a social worker and teacher who started a speaking business with Laurie Young at their world headquarters in Decatur, Michigan. Kay continues to adventure as she ages. p. 144, 161, 189

Vikki Claflin lives in Hood River, Oregon, where she writes the award-winning humor blog Laugh Lines. She believes laughter, a good glass of wine, and an econo-sized box of Milk Duds are the path to true Zen. She's written for the Michael J. Fox Foundation, Erma Bombeck's Writer's Workshop, The Huffington Post, Scary Mommy, Generation Fabulous, Midlife Boulevard, Better After 50, and *Funny Times* magazine. She received a "Voices of the Year" humor award and released her book *Shake, Rattle & Roll with It: Living and Laughing with Parkinson's.* p. 104, 173

Your Glasses Are on Top of Your Head

Jean Di Carlo-Wagner, M.A., is a yoga teacher trainer, activist ,and advocate for Yoga for Cancer Survivors. She is also a writer for *CURE* magazine, and secretly desires to make life funnier and fuller. She can be reached at YogaBeing.net. p. 213

Mary Drago is a Cancer Registrar in Connecticut, married almost forty years to the same man, and has three cats. She loves to read, cook, watch old movies, drink coffee, and sit on her Adirondack chair on the porch where she can look out at nature. p. 39, 196

Bahgat Elsagher is the father of two fantastic grown children, and he hangs out with Brenda a lot—for about thirty years now. p. 149, 195

Joyce Elsen enjoys community volunteer work, traveling, baking, and spending time with friends and family, especially her children and grandchildren. p. 20

Rick Elsen is the owner of Lakemaps and enjoys life at the lake and traveling the world. He delightfully says, "I'm just an old guy with a hot trophy wife." p. 109

Laurie Fabrizio is a writer who resides in Medina, Minnesota. She has also been published in *The Talking Stick Anthology, A Long Story Short, Simple Joy, Mom Writer's Literary Magazine*, and *Humor Press's America's Funniest Humor*. p. 88, 205

Tanya Fuad is a playwright whose plays have been produced in theaters in San Diego. She is currently working on a new play addressing the dire situation of refugees called *Camp Life*. She draws on her experience as a health coordinator for Save the Children. Tanya also enjoys hiking in the mountains and swimming in the ocean. p. 193

Roberta Gold is a Recreation Therapist and a Humor Therapist. She created her company, Laughter for the Health of It, with a mission to empower everyone to have a more positive outlook. She is an author, gives uplifting workshops and keynotes, and is currently teaching students how to use humor instead of violence to be more resilient. p. 41

Pamela Goldstein became a prolific and seasoned writer during her twenty years as a nurse, and then fifteen years as a radio show producer/host. Her work can be found in over fifteen anthology books, including many in the Chicken Soup for the Soul series. Pam's play, *The Interview*, has been workshopped and is now being considered for an off-Broadway production. An acclaimed editor as well, Pam edited the Chicken Soup book *O Canada: The Wonders of Winter.* p. 77, 157

T'Mara Goodsell is an award-winning multi-genre writer and teacher who lives near St. Louis, Missouri. She has written for various anthologies, newspapers, and publications, and is working on a book for young adults. p. 92

Kathryn Hammer's real talent is helping people find their authentic voices for sparkling and successful communication. Finding lost items is just a sideline for her. Visit her at keynotecafe.com. p. 53

Chris Heeter is a leadership speaker, wilderness guide, and poet. Her business, The Wild Institute, helps people be more *wild* at work and in the rest of their lives. As the story attests, she's had terrific *wild* role models in her mom and grandmother. p. 114

Kathryn Holmes is retired and lives in Minnetonka, Minnesota, with her husband, Charlie. Her book, entitled *I Stand with Courage: One Woman's Journey to Conquer Paralysis*, is an inspiration to all. She can be reached through her website IStandWithCourage.com. p. 24

Judith Huck says she has the good fortune of being a wife, mother of three, and grandmother of eight. She is continually amazed by the evolution of technology from the four-inch Hallicrafter black-and-white TV with the six-inch magnifying glass she grew up watching, to the cell phones and, of course, iPads of today. Judith is a native Minnesotan. p. 13

Maxine Jeffris is a comedian, writer, cat lover, and painter of walls and, sometimes, floors. She often appears in local theaters, sitting toward the back, close to an exit. p. 75, 121

Cheryl Jobe is now settled on a raw piece of hillside with her dear husband of over forty years, three dogs, and a horse. The long years of being town-bound are over, and she's content. Her advice: Don't wait for your dreams to become reality. Chase them down and tackle them. p. 27, 83

Jeanette Kane is from Bemidji in northern Minnesota, where she met and married her college sweetheart. They have two wonderful children and four amazing grandchildren. She loves to sew and work in the yard, and play the piano, accordion, and organ. p. 51

Carol Larson was awarded for "Women Who Have Broken Barriers for Colorectal Cancer in 2008." In 2013, she was appointed to the national Affiliated Support Group board of the United Ostomy Association of America (UOAA) and in 2014 wrote a book, *Positive Options for Colorectal Cancer*, available at TurnerBooks.com. She lives in Minnesota with her husband, Dave. p. 131

Brian R. Lee is a freelance writer and former journalist who recently retired from the railroad industry. Besides magazine and newspaper articles, he also authored a book, *For the Love of Cars*, and has a couple other books in the works. p. 141, 164

Rae Ellen Lee plans to grow old much later in life, or maybe not at all (as quoted from Patty Carey, rodeo rider, in 1901). She writes humor, fiction, and neurotica. Her books include *My Next Husband Will Be Normal* and *A Field Guide to Geezers*. Read more at raeellenlee.com. p. 190

Barbara Kelley Linkous was born in Linesville, Pennsylvania, and is a graduate of Avila College, with her B.A. in religious studies, with honors. She worked at JB White and Associates, was an H&R Block tax preparer, and retired in 1996. She has a daughter named Georga, after her husband George who passed away in 2009. p. 37

Red Lyons is seventy-eight, short and getting shorter, and balding, which is a grandiose term for bald. Remember, Grandma Moses was even older when she became famous; however, she was talented, which helped. One of his grandkids guessed he was over a hundred, but she was probably just judging on his appearance. p. 18

Linda MacNeal is a professional speaker and produces therapeutic humor workshops teaching people how to use humor to reduce stress and increase productivity. Visit her website, Humorsolutions.com. p. 209

Lisa Millham is a hospice nurse by day and fantasy novelist by night who writes under the name Elisabeth Hamill. She is a colon cancer survivor, and lives in the wilds of eastern suburban Kansas with her family, fending off flying monkey attacks and prepping for the zombie apocalypse. p. 9

Eileen Mitchell is an award-winning writer with recognition from Thurber House, the Will Rogers Writers' Workshop, and the Robert Benchley Society. She's a contributing author to many books, including Chicken Soup for the Soul and *Bedpan Banter*, and currently writes the Film Hound blog for the *Seattle Post*. p. 73

Marsha Warren Mittman was originally editor of an international company's in-house magazine, and has recently returned to writing after a long hiatus. A chapbook has been published, and numerous poems and short stories have appeared (or are forthcoming) in various literary magazines and anthologies including two Chicken Soup for the Soul books: *Time to Thrive* and *Volunteering/ Giving Back*. A native New Yorker, Mittman lives in South Dakota and is the recipient of seven Midwest writing awards. p. 137, 151

Mary Kay Morrison is an educator who has taught at virtually every level of the educational spectrum, as well as facilitating keynote presentations and workshop sessions for the past thirty years. She is president of the Association of Applied and Therapeutic Humor (AATH) board, and founded the AATH Humor Academy graduate studies program. Visit her at questforhumor.com. p. 58

Alice Murphy has roots in Iowa and wings in Minnesota. She is the baby sister to nine, mom to two, and grandma to four. She says she is "Still dodging Iowa jokes, and laughing at myself—and laughing with friends." p. 212

Karel Murray is a motivational humorist, communication/ leadership strategist, and author. Her extensive business experience and professional speaking background combine for an incredible attendee experience. Information about Karel can be found at www.Karel.com, or you can contact her directly at karel@karel.com. p. 65

Linda O'Connell writes from St. Louis. She has been published in twenty-two Chicken Soup for the Soul books, *Bed Pan Banter*, and more than a hundred anthologies, magazines, books, and online publications. She loves dark chocolate and the beach. p. 66

Bob Ramsey is a lifelong educator, freelance writer, and advocate for Vital Aging Network. He and his wife reside in St. Louis Park, Minnesota. p. 126

Renee Rongen is an award-winning author of *Grandy's Quilt* and *Fundamentally Female*. She's also an entrepreneur who engages her audiences to live life at full throttle. For more information about Renee, go to www.reneerongen.com. p. 183

Dorothy Rosby is a syndicated humor columnist whose work appears in eleven western and midwestern states, as well as in several magazines. She is the author of the humor book, *I Used to Think I Was Not That Bad and Then I Got to Know Me Better.* p. 98

Joyce Saltman is Professor Emeritus of Special Education at Southern Connecticut State University in New Haven. She has two hilarious kids and a very funny husband, and has been a humorous motivational speaker since 1983. She donates all her speaking engagement fees to favorite charities, and ultimately hopes to die laughing— but not too soon. p. 16

Marilyn Speiker grew up on a farm in Jordan, Minnesota, with one sister and ten brothers. She moved to a town nearby when she married, worked for the city, and retired twelve years ago. With three children, four grandchildren, and six great-grandchildren, all living within thirty minutes of her, she stays busy. For other fun, she enjoys teaching line dancing for the lovely ladies ages sixty to eighty. p. 63

Rox Tarrant is an exceptional comedian and extraordinary producer of comedy shows. Rox has been making audiences laugh for twenty years with her original, heartfelt, and relevant humor. "Ever since I was a young girl, I wanted to be a comedian; now that I'm a comedian, I just want to be a young girl!" p. 171

Edna L. Thayer, CLL, a.k.a. "The Laughing Lady," is co-author of an award-winning book, *A Mirthful Spirit: Embracing Laughter for Wellness.* She has given over eight hundred talks on the subject of laughter in seventeen different states plus Canada, and calls her business "Humor THAYER-apy." p. 204

Deborah Tompkins is a cancer survivor, and she lives with her adult son, who has autism. She has a master's degree in human development. Her freelance writing focuses on the Boomer generation, and busting the traditional myths and stereotypes of aging. p. 177

Dan Van Oss grew up reading about everything he could borrow from the town library, although admittedly sometimes just to get the sticker segments so he could complete the Reading Centipede for each book he finished. You can catch his weekly humor column, *The Dubious Knowledge Institute*, at danvanoss.com. p. 200

Sherry Wenborg is a mother of three and grandmother to four. She and her husband, Doug, just celebrated their fifty-first anniversary. She loves to line dance, travel, and enjoys book club. She enjoys her affiliation with Philanthropic Educational Organization (PEO), which provides education grants for women at Cottey College in Missouri. p. 117

Michele Wood is a rich, bold, full-bodied veteran RN who hits a keyboard or the road, sharing stories of resilience, courage, and character. Witty and wise, her strength, experience, and perspective promise inspiration and lots of laughter. p. 100

Laurie Young is a counselor and teacher who speaks with Kay Caskey on the adventures of laughter and positive aging. Together they have taught over a hundred thousand people how to juggle, and both are life-long laughers. p. 144, 161

Discussion Questions

1. Could you relate to the title of this book?

2. After reading the acknowledgments, do you think it's possible to age hilariously? What part of aging is serious for you?

3. Do you have friends in your life who are older than you who look at life with humor? How does this affect their lives?

4. Do you worry about aging and how others will view you?

5. What scares you the most? What brings you calm about aging?

6. What are you looking forward to as you get older?

7. What was your earliest perspective on aging? What do you remember thinking about people older than you?

8. Have you or someone you loved experienced menopause and was your experience different or relatable to the examples in this book?

9. What are three outstanding desires you have to fulfill in your life?

10. Do you have regrets about your life? If you could change them, what would you do?

11. What has been most important to you as you age?

12. Did any of these stories bring about a happy or teaching memory for you?

13. My favorite story was _____ because _____.

14. Was there an overall theme in this book that stuck out to you?

15. Is it comforting to know other people are aging with similarities?

16. If you could add a perspective of aging to this book, what story would you tell?

17. When did you realize you were getting older?

18. Do you laugh about aging? Did any story in this book make you laugh out loud?

If you have a personal story you would like to share, the author is eager to consider it for the next edition of *Your Glasses Are on Top of Your Head*. Send your submission to **brenda@livingandlaughing.com**.

About Brenda Elsagher

Brenda Elsagher is a national motivational speaker, author, and comedian. She is the author of five books, *If the Battle Is Over, Why Am I Still in Uniform?*, *I'd Like to Buy a Bowel Please!*, *Bedpan Banter*, *It's in the Bag and Under the Covers*, and most recently, *Your Glasses Are on Top of Your Head*.

**Book Brenda for an event at your location!
Presentations include:**

Humor and Adversity . . . Bring It On!

Humor is like breath . . . it's needed at work, home, and play. Brenda dares audiences to laugh about taboo subjects

and challenges them to dig deeper for the gems that need excavating.

Humor and Healing From the Patient's Perspective

Who knew a patient could teach something new to health care professionals? A rare look "behind the scenes" with humorous insights, they will walk away assured they make a difference in their patients' lives.

Coping With Cancer

A journey of laughter with a respite from the realities of life with cancer. Daring to say things that people never say, Brenda relates to her audience in the language of people in the cancer trenches.

Your Glasses Are on Top of Your Head: Tales of Life, Longevity, and Laughter

Brenda shows audiences how to find the funny in the little things. This talk shows how important it is to use humor to stay engaged in the business of living, and how to be grateful for being on the top side of the grass.

Office: 952-882-9882
Email: Brenda@livingandlaughing.com
Website: LivingAndLaughing.com